# ‹ZIMBABWE›

# MAJOR WORLD NATIONS

# ZIMBABWE

Patricia Barnes-Svarney

CHELSEA HOUSE PUBLISHERS
Philadelphia

Chelsea House Publishers

*Contributing Author:* James Rhoderick

Copyright © 1999 by Chelsea House Publishers,
a division of Main Line Book Co.
All rights reserved.
Printed and bound in the United States of America.

First Printing

1  3  5  7  9  8  6  4  2

Library of Congress Cataloging-in-Publication Data

Barnes-Svarney, Patricia L.
Zimbabwe / Patricia Barnes-Svarney.
p.   cm. — (Major world nations)
Includes index.
ISBN 0–7910–4753–9
1. Zimbabwe—Juvenile literature.
I. Title.   II. Series.
IN PROCESS
968.91—dc21   97–18122
CIP
AC

# ◄CONTENTS►

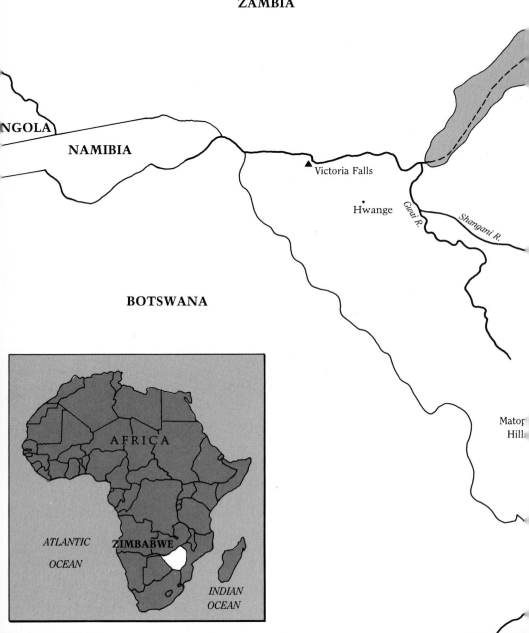

**ZAMBIA**

**NGOLA**

**NAMIBIA**

▲ Victoria Falls

Hwange

*Guai R.*

*Shangani R.*

**BOTSWANA**

Mator
Hill:

AFRICA

*ATLANTIC*

*OCEAN*

**ZIMBABWE**

*INDIAN*
*OCEAN*

# ◄ FACTS AT A GLANCE ►

### Land and People

| | |
|---|---|
| Area | 150,820 square miles (392,132 square kilometers) |
| Population | 11,300,000 |
| Population Density | 75 people per square mile (29 per square kilometer) |
| Population Distribution | Rural, 69 percent; urban, 31 percent |
| Capital | Harare (population 1,200,000) |
| Other Cities | Bulawayo (population 621,000); Chitungwiza (population 274,000); Mutare (population 132,000) |
| Highest Point | Mt. Inyangani, 8,517 feet (2,593 meters) |
| Major Rivers | Zambezi, Limpopo, Shangani, Lundi, Sabi |
| Major Lake | Kariba |
| Official Language | English |
| Other Languages | Chishona, Sindebele, Batwa |
| Ethnic Groups | Shona-speaking Bantu, 71 percent; Ndebele-speaking Bantu, 16 percent; white, 1 percent; other (including Asian), 12 percent |
| Religions | Syncretic (blend of Christian and traditional beliefs), 50 percent; Christian (Anglican, Catholic, African Christian), 25 percent; animist, 24 percent; other, 1 percent |
| Life Expectancy | Women, 42 years; men, 42 years |

# Economy

| | |
|---|---|
| Land Use | Forest, 49 percent; meadows and pastures, 13 percent; farming, 7 percent; other, 31 percent |
| Labor Force | Agriculture, 70 percent; manufacturing, 17 percent; mining, 7 percent; other, 6 percent |
| Major Agricultural Products | Tobacco, beef, cotton, corn, sugar, milk, wheat, coffee, soybeans, palm oil |
| Major Manufacturing Products | Metals, chemicals and petroleum products, textiles, clothing and shoes, cigarettes, beverages and processed foods |
| Principal Exports | Tobacco, gold, asbestos, nickel, cotton, sugar, corn |
| Principal Imports | Machinery, iron and steel, petroleum, consumer goods |
| Currency | Zimbabwe dollar (equal to about U.S. $0.09) |
| Average Household Income | Z $9,164 |
| Average Household Expenses | Food, 21 percent; clothing and shoes, 12 percent; alcohol and tobacco, 11 percent; travel, 8 percent; housing, 9 percent; utilities and fuel; 8 percent; furniture and household supplies, 7 percent; education, 5 percent; medicines, 3 percent; health services, 2 percent; books and newspapers, 2 percent |

# Government

| | |
|---|---|
| Form of Government | Parliamentary democracy |
| Parliament | House of Assembly with 150 members, 120 of whom are elected |
| Head of Government | Executive President |

| | |
|---|---|
| Major Political Parties | ZANU (Zimbabwe African National Union), ZANU-Ndonga, CAZ (Conservative Alliance of Zimbabwe) |
| Eligibility to Vote | All men and women over the age of 18 |
| Administrative Provinces | Matabeleland North, Matabeleland South, Masvingo, Midlands, Manicaland, Mashonaland, Mashonaland Center, Mashonaland East |

# ◄HISTORY AT A GLANCE►

| | |
|---|---|
| **200 to 1000 A.D.** | Bantu peoples from the north settle in southeast Africa. |
| **1100 to 1700** | The city-state known as Great Zimbabwe is built and ruled by successive Bantu empires. |
| **1855** | The Scottish missionary-explorer David Livingstone visits and names Victoria Falls. |
| **1871** | Karl Mauch visits and describes the ruins of Great Zimbabwe. |
| **1885** | Lobengula, king of the Ndebele, signs the Rudd Concession, unknowingly giving mineral rights in Mashonaland to Cecil Rhodes. |
| **1890** | Cecil Rhodes sends the British South African Company's Pioneer Column into Mashonaland; it is the first occupation of the country by the British. |
| **1891** | Britain declares Rhodesia a British protectorate. |
| **1896** | Shona and Ndebele tribes stage an unsuccessful uprising against the Europeans. The protectorate is divided into Northern Rhodesia and Southern Rhodesia. |
| **1902** | Rhodes dies and is buried at Matopos Hills. |
| **1923** | Great Britain annexes Southern Rhodesia as a colony. |

1953    With Northern Rhodesia and Nyasaland, South-
        ern Rhodesia enters the Federation of Rhodesia
        and Nyasaland.

1964    Ian Smith becomes prime minister, breaks off
        relations with Britain, and announces Rhode-
        sia's Unilateral Declaration of Independence.

1966    The civil war begins with ZANU's first major
        raid on the white population.

1970    Rhodesia becomes a republic under Smith's
        prowhite government. Black nationalist activity
        and guerrilla fighting increase.

1979    Smith agrees to accept a new constitution.
        Elections are held, and blacks win 80 percent of
        parliamentary seats. Robert Mugabe, leader of
        ZANU, is elected prime minister.

1980    Rhodesia becomes fully independent as Zim-
        babwe, ruled by the black majority.

| | |
|---|---|
| **1982** | Hostility between ZANU and ZAPU parties, and the Shona and Ndebele, considered a "state of emergency." |
| **1985** | The Five-Year Plan is put into effect to boost the economy and convert to a socialist state. |
| **1989** | ZANU and ZAPU merge, ending the state of emergency. |
| **1991** | Economic Structural Adjustment Program introduces a market-based economy. |
| **1992** | Severe drought strikes. The government asks outside donors for famine aid. |
| **1996** | An estimated one-tenth of the population have HIV, the virus that causes AIDS. |

*These founders of the political party ZANU led the fight for independence in the 1960s and 1970s. Robert Mugabe, third from right, is president today.*

*A modern painting shows how gold was mined and sold by the Zimbabwean trading empires. Women work in the caves; men wash the gold in a stream; and, at the top, a chieftain barters with an Arab trader.*

# Zimbabwe
# and the World

Located in the heart of southern Africa, the Republic of Zimbabwe was described by the British poet Rudyard Kipling as a "land washed by the sun"—wide, open spaces in the west and lush green mountains in the east. It is a fortunate land filled with abundant wildlife and many natural wonders. Yet it is also a suffering land. Racial strife began a century ago. A 15-year war of independence ended in 1980 with 27,000 dead. Hardship, poverty, and even starvation haunt the population of 11,300,000, most of whom are farmers and laborers. In the two decades since independence a plague of HIV, the virus that causes AIDS, has also swept through the nation.

For centuries, the area now known as Zimbabwe has been economically important to Africa and the world. Early groups of native African peoples mined gold and traded the precious metal to countries such as China and India. In the late 1800s, white European settlers, most of them British, immigrated to the country. They became important producers of crops such as tea and tobacco and minerals such as gold and tin. Today countries on Zimbabwe's border depend on the Zimbabwean railroads for importing and exporting goods. Zimbabwe's extensive mineral resources are important to

*Rhodesian whites moved the blacks into walled "protected villages."*

world production. For example, the country is one of the world's major sources of the mineral chromium.

Politically, the area known as Zimbabwe has undergone many changes over the years. Before the immigration of the white settlers, native African groups fought each other for control of the land. In the 1880s, the European settlers claimed the country, which they called Rhodesia, as their own. The African peoples fought to keep control of their homeland, but the settlers won the confrontation. White rule continued for almost 70 years, during which time Rhodesia was a British colony.

In 1953, the Rhodesian government changed the colony's name to Southern Rhodesia and joined the Federation of Rhodesia and Nyasaland, which consisted of three former British colonies in Africa. When the other two former colonies dissolved the federation to form independent African nations governed by their black African populations, Southern Rhodesia changed its name back to Rhodesia. Led by Prime Minister Ian Smith, the white ruling party declared Rhodesia independent. The white minority, however, was determined not to let the government of Rhodesia be controlled by the majority of the population—the black Africans.

Many nations protested Smith's action and wanted Rhodesia to be governed by its black majority. Member countries of the United Nations showed their disapproval of continued white rule in Rhodesia by supporting economic sanctions against Rhodesia—that is, by reducing or eliminating trade, refusing either to buy Rhodesian products or to sell goods to the Rhodesians.

Inside the country, political conflict between blacks and whites caused problems for the white minority ruling government. In riots and terrorist skirmishes, government forces clashed with black African nationalists—blacks who passionately believed that their native country should be run by the black majority. Pressure from Rhodesian blacks and world opinion eventually forced the white ruling Rhodesian government to change its position. In 1980, Rhodesia

*Prince Charles of Great Britain (center) attended a formal dinner on the eve of independence.*

became the Republic of Zimbabwe, a democratic republic governed by majority vote.

Despite victory in the struggle for majority rule, political strife continued in Zimbabwe for nearly a decade. The two major black parties were supported by two rival populations, the Shona-speaking and the Ndebele-speaking peoples, who had a long history of war and competition. In the late 1980s the two parties, ZAPU and ZANU, merged into one ruling party with Robert Mugabe as head, and the ethnic conflicts dissipated. Zimbabwe's consolidated government now faces little organized political opposition.

Mugabe's government emerged from the waning years of the Cold War with a socialist plan, one in which the state owned and administered land and factories, fixed prices and wages, and provided subsidized jobs in the civil service and elsewhere. This plan proved untimely during the worldwide free-market development of the early 1990s. Since 1991, a new economic adjustment program has attempted to remove price and currency controls, allow for more private enterprise and diversity, and attract foreign investment.

Until the collapse of the Soviet Union, Zimbabwe maintained relations with both the East and West. Today, as majority rule has at last come to South Africa and communism has withered elsewhere, Zimbabwe is poised to play a prominent role in the economic and political development of Africa, becoming closely involved with the Organization of African Unity, the European Union, the World Bank, and the United Nations.

Zimbabwe has many resources, including minerals, forests, and water for hydroelectric plants. But drought, huge deficits, famine, and disease are hurting the government's ability to provide education, employment, and health care for the people. Zimbabwe also faces high interest on international loans. Though tribal disputes and political infighting no longer cripple the country, the painful transition to open markets has brought much hardship. More ominously, experts fear that the true extent of the AIDS epidemic in Zimbabwe and elsewhere in Africa is yet to be seen.

With all of these problems, can a politically organized, more urbanized, and internationally ambitious Zimbabwe find the prosperity necessary to move beyond them?

*Victoria Falls, the "smoke that thunders," is one of the world's most magnificent natural wonders, twice as high as Niagara Falls in North America.*

# Tabletop Country

Zimbabwe's geography can be traced to the very beginnings of Africa. Geologists believe that Africa was once part of a supercontinent called Gondwanaland. This huge landmass began to break up more than 180 million years ago because of continental drift—the process that causes large pieces of the earth's crust to twist and turn as they are dragged slowly across the planet's surface by the internal forces of heat and gravity. As the once-connected continents of Africa and South America separated, the Atlantic Ocean filled the widening gap. Africa has remained a separate continent ever since.

As the African plate moved, many changes took place on the continent. Great rift zones began to form—giant tears in the land, such as those at the Red Sea and the Great Rift Valley in Kenya. Mountains, volcanoes, plateaus, and rivers also were formed as the continent shifted. In Zimbabwe, large fractures tore the rocks apart. Deep in the earth, hot molten rock worked its way to the surface. The land buckled, forming the mountains and the large wall-like escarpments, or cliffs, seen in northern and eastern Zimbabwe. The lifting up of the land created a huge, flat plateau in the center of the country, giving it the nickname "Tabletop Country."

*Steep granite cliffs called escarpments border the High Veld.*

The rocks of Zimbabwe are some of the oldest on earth. They are from the geologic time period called the Pre-Cambrian ("before life") and were formed more than 2.5 billion years ago. (The earth is estimated to be 4.6 billion years old.) Many of the rocks are granites and basalts; they were formed when hot rock cooled quickly at the earth's surface. Other rocks, called schists, were affected by the intense heat and pressure associated with the movement of the continent.

Zimbabwe is located in southeastern Africa. It is south of the equator and more than 100 miles (161 kilometers) north of the Tropic of Capricorn. The landlocked country measures 150,820 square miles (392,132 square kilometers), making it about the size of the state of California in the United States. The greatest distance from north to south is 460 miles (740 kilometers) and from east to west is 540 miles (869 kilometers).

Zimbabwe borders five other African nations. In the west, it touches a tip of Namibia, which gained its independence from South Africa in 1990. To the north is Zambia; the Zambezi River is the boundary between the two countries. To the south, the Limpopo River makes close to 100 miles (161 kilometers) of the boundary between Zimbabwe and South Africa. To the east is Mozambique, with the Indian Ocean 150 miles (241 kilometers) away on its far side. To the southwest is Botswana.

The land may be divided into three regions based on altitude, or height above sea level. Areas more than 4,000 feet (1,220 meters) above sea level are called High Veld; this makes up about a fifth of the country and forms the Central Plateau, a high, flat plateau that runs from northeast to southwest. The second region is the Middle Veld. It is between 2,000 and 4,000 feet (610 and 1,220 meters) above sea level. This region surrounds the High Veld. The last region, the Low Veld, includes the parts of the country that are less than 2,000 feet (610 meters) above sea level. The Low Veld is hot and receives little rainfall. Diseases such as malaria are common in the Low Veld, which is the least populated region.

Another way to describe Zimbabwe's geography is to divide the country into the eastern highlands, including the Inyanga Mountains, and the western savanna plateau. The rolling mountains of the east run along the border of Zimbabwe and Mozambique. Because of the heavy annual rainfall, Zimbabwe's eastern highlands are one of the most agriculturally productive regions in Africa. Large orchards, tea fields, and timber plantations dot the mountainsides.

*The grass-covered western savanna, with clumps of open, parklike vegetation, is home to large herds of game animals such as gazelles—and to the lions that prey upon them.*

*The hilly eastern highlands are one of Africa's most fertile regions.*

And the green scenic hills have long been a favorite retreat of vacationers and tourists. The highest elevation is Mt. Inyangani, near the eastern border. It rises 8,517 feet (2,593 meters) above sea level.

The lowest elevations are on the plateau to the west and average 2,000 feet (610 meters) above sea level. This western region is called the savanna plateau. The savanna is relatively flat, open or parklike land dotted with small shrubs and bushes that grow in its rich brown-red soil.

The savanna is vital to the people and the wildlife of Zimbabwe. People live on the savanna by grazing cattle and raising crops. Wild animals need the savanna as a food source. Grazing animals depend on its grasses, and in turn predators feed on them. For example, whereas a lion's survival on the savanna depends on its catch of gazelles, elephants, gazelles, and other creatures need the vegetation that the savanna offers.

## Natural Wonders and Resources

In the southwest, near Zimbabwe's second largest city, Bulawayo, lie the Matopos Hills—a large tract of low hills covered with isolated granite boulders. The Matopos Hills cover more than 12 square miles

(31 square kilometers). Over thousands of years, wind and rain have carved the boulders into strange shapes. The larger boulders, some of which are the size of a house, dwarf the local wildlife—even the elephants. Some rocks are piled up like oddly shaped building blocks; a few look as if one good push could send them tumbling to the ground.

The Matopos Hills are sacred ground to the native African peoples of Zimbabwe. Bushmen who lived in the area more than 2,000 years ago drew pictures on cave walls and rocks at Matopos Hills. The drawings show their way of life, including hunting and domestic scenes. Many great chiefs of ancient tribes and communities are buried in the Hills.

Northwest of Harare, the capital of Zimbabwe, are the Chinhoyi Caves—among the most dramatic geologic features in northeast Zimbabwe. Long ago, when parts of a bed of limestone rock collapsed, several giant holes and caves were formed. Eventually, the holes were filled with water. One pool, called the Sleeping Pool, is more than 328 feet (100 meters) deep. The water is so clear that

*The boulder-strewn Matopos Hills were once a sacred burying ground.*

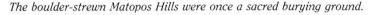

*A rock painting near Harare shows early hunters in pursuit of hippos, buffalo, and antelope.*

rock layers and fish can be seen far below the surface of the pool. Near the pools are the caves. Numerous ancient stone tools that have been found in the caves show that these natural shelters were used centuries ago.

The savanna is rich in mineral deposits, including gold, copper, chromium, and iron ore. Gold was mined by the ancient Monomotapa civilization, which sold the precious metal to the Chinese, Indians, and Indonesians centuries ago.

In southern Africa, water is a very important resource. Zimbabwe has many dams and reservoirs, which provide water for irrigation and drinking. Most of the larger cities have several dam sites that supply water to residents, factories, and nearby farms. There are more than half a dozen dams around Bulawayo, including the Umzingwane and the Khami Railway dams.

Zimbabwe is fortunate to have many great rivers: the Zambezi in the north; the Shangani in the west; the Sabi and the Odzi in the east; and the Limpopo in the south. Several large lakes dot the land. The largest is Lake Kariba.

The Zambezi is the best-known river in Zimbabwe. It travels more than 2,200 miles (3,540 kilometers), from its start in Zaire, through Angola and Zambia to the border of Zimbabwe, then through Mozambique and on to the Indian Ocean. Along the border between Zimbabwe and Zambia, the river passes through two exceptional sites: Victoria Falls and man-made Lake Kariba.

Victoria Falls is made up of four waterfalls and is located in northwest Zimbabwe. The falls are the Eastern Cataract, the Rainbow Falls, the Main Falls, and the Boiling Pot. At their highest point, the falls are 343 feet (105 meters) high. They are almost twice as high and one and one-half times as wide as Niagara Falls in the United States. The falls were known by the native Kololo people centuries ago and were called *mosi-oa-tunya*, or "smoke that thunders"—an appropriate name because the sound of the water tumbling into the deep gorge below can be heard up to 10 miles (16 kilometers) from the falls, and the spray can be seen up to 40 miles (64 kilometers) away. The first white man to see the falls was David Livingstone, the Scottish explorer, who named the raging falls for Queen Victoria of England.

Lake Kariba, one of the largest man-made lakes in the world, is held back by the Kariba Dam, one of the world's largest dams. The dam was built across the Zambezi River in the late 1950s to supply electrical power to factories and mines of the two growing nations of Northern Rhodesia (now Zambia) and Southern Rhodesia (now Zimbabwe). The dam has the potential to produce 8,500 million kilowatt-hours of electricity per year.

The building of the dam caused many changes. Before the land was flooded, families whose ancestors had lived along that part of the river had to be moved. The wildlife in the area had to be saved. "Operation Noah" was conducted at the site to carry or chase the wildlife in the area to higher ground. Today the lake covers 2,000 square miles (5,180 square kilometers).

Northeast of Lake Kariba is the Mana Pools National Park—a large collection of shallow pools. The pools, which extend for more than 44 miles (708 kilometers) along the Zambezi River, were formed when the river changed course. As erosion or flooding directed the flow into a new channel, traces of the old channel remained. Filled with water, they became small pools.

The Mana Pools National Park is more than 965 square miles (2,500 square kilometers) in area. The park is one of Zimbabwe's largest wildlife habitats and contains a great variety of plant life. More than 8,000 elephants, 16,000 buffalo, and a struggling population of some of the world's last remaining black rhinoceros live in a part of the park called the Middle Valley. Other animals include a large number of waterfowl and woodland birds.

The eastern and western parts of Zimbabwe have different soils. The nutrient-rich soil of the east comes from the weathered rock of the eastern highlands. In the late 1800s and early 1900s, farms in the eastern highlands were so productive that Rhodesia was known as the "breadbasket of Africa." Farmers in the western savanna do not grow as many different types of crops as farmers in the eastern highlands; the soil is not as rich, and there is much less rain. But the soil of the savanna is perfect for growing the grass needed to graze cattle, sheep, and goats.

Many different plants cover the highlands and savanna. In the east, the grasses are lush and green most of the year, and such flowers as the wild scarlet flame lily—the national flower—bring color to the countryside. The western savanna is covered with coarse grasses, bushes, and trees.

The savanna has very few trees. Like most vegetation in dry regions, the trees of western Zimbabwe often store water to survive the dry months of the year. The baobab tree is one such tree. It is tall and thick, with thousands of short, thin branches that look as if they should be the roots of the tree. African legend says that once in anger the gods uprooted the baobab and put them back in the ground upside down. The fruit of the *marula*, another tree common in the savanna, is a favorite food of elephants.

*The stocky baobab tree, with its tiny branches, is a familiar silhouette on the savanna.*

Zimbabwe is a wildlife lover's dream: Several vast tracts of land and many smaller areas have been set aside as parks and reserves. Large herds of wild animals roam free in their natural state. Almost all of the animals, even those once thought to be on the brink of extinction, are protected by the parks.

The people of Zimbabwe know the value of keeping the wild animals free. In the late 1800s and early 1900s, thousands of animals were killed by hunters in search of ivory, skins, and animal trophies. Many species of wildlife became scarce; others, like the white rhinoceros, all but disappeared.

By the 1950s the government realized that sanctuaries had to be set aside. Zimbabwe now has one of the highest concentrations of wild animals in Africa, including elephants, rhinoceroses, gorillas, lions, leopards, zebras, jackals, hippopotamuses, chimpanzees, gazelles, baboons, impalas, lynxes, and dozens of smaller animals—more than 40 species of grazing and meat-eating animals. A few of the wildlife sanctuaries are devoted to protecting the thousands of animals that migrate through Zimbabwe at various times of the year and breed in the spring. Hwange National Park, near Victoria Falls, is the largest wildlife sanctuary in Zimbabwe. It has more than 7,000 elephants, packs of wild dogs, and dozens of varieties of birds (including ostriches), reptiles, and insects. Other sanctuaries are the Gona-Re-Zhou National Park in the south and the Matusadona National Park to the north.

Crocodiles infest parts of Zimbabwe. These large reptiles are very dangerous. More people are killed each year by crocodiles than by any other animal on the savanna. Snakes and lizards are common also, and more than 500 species of birds have been spotted.

Fisheries have been established on the numerous lakes and rivers in Zimbabwe. These freshwater fisheries are a source of protein-rich fish—an important food source, as the diet of most Africans consists mainly of starches. It is not unusual to see hundreds of people fishing on the shores of Lake Kariba. The lake supports an ample supply of fish for local people and for fish markets in the larger cities and towns to the south.

## Climate and Weather

Zimbabwe has a warm and comfortable climate, defined as moderate subtropical. Although the country is located in the world's tropical zone, its height above sea level keeps it from having a hot, steamy, truly tropical climate. The climate is pleasant because it is so constant—there is little change from season to season.

Weather in Zimbabwe has been compared to the United States's middle California or the lowlands of Switzerland in Europe: cool nights, moderate days, and plenty of sun. The prevailing winds in Zimbabwe travel from east to west; most of them come off the Indian Ocean. Because Zimbabwe is south of the equator, its summer is from December to early March, and its short, dry winter is from June to September.

Temperatures average between 68 and 77 degrees Fahrenheit (20 to 25 degrees Centigrade) in the winter and around 77 degrees Fahrenheit (25 degrees Centigrade) in the summer. The average day has about 7.5 hours of sunshine. Zimbabwe's peak rainfall occurs during the summer months. On the average, rainfall in the east is 40 to 80 inches (1,000 to 2,000 millimeters) per year; in the west, it is 20 to 40 inches (500 to 1,000 millimeters) per year. Rainfall can

*This farmer's donkey was one of thousands of victims of a severe drought in 1966.*

be reduced by as much as 25 percent if the country is experiencing a drought.

Like many other African countries, Zimbabwe experiences droughts—prolonged periods when the rains cease to freshen the land and help crops to grow. Droughts are nothing new to the people of Zimbabwe, but they are always difficult to cope with. Wildlife and farm animals die because of the lack of water. Fields become parched and brown. It is not unusual to see whole villages abandoned, their inhabitants gone to search for water. No one really knows what causes a drought. Some scientists blame human activity, such as the cutting down of forests. Others say droughts are caused by the natural long-term change of the desert regions or changes in the global weather patterns.

For centuries, Zimbabwe's geography has been a balance between land, climate, wildlife, and people. It is a delicate balance, one that must be nurtured in the years to come.

Great Zimbabwe has fascinated and puzzled travelers and historians for more than a century. These "houses of stone" gave the country its present name.

# Cities of Stone

Some of the earliest chapters of human history were written in Zimbabwe. They can be read in the fossil record of Zimbabwe's ancient rocks. More than 14 million years ago, a small woodland creature roamed the lands that are now called India, China, and Turkey. It also wandered through eastern and southern Africa. This species, called *Ramapithecus* (Rama's ape) by paleontologists (scientists who study fossils), is believed to be one of the first human ancestors. Scientists also believe that Rama's ape lived in the region that is now Zimbabwe for more than 7 million years.

There is a gap in the African fossil record for the next 4 million years or so. But another humanlike fossil, about 3.5 million years old, was found in 1973 in Tanzania. Scientists began to piece together a new picture of human origins. They now believe that around 2 million years ago two kinds of hominid (manlike) species lived in eastern Africa. The two species stood almost upright and shared the lush green grasslands that then covered most of eastern Africa.

One species, called *Homo habilis* by paleontologists, was a slender and agile creature who walked almost like modern man. *Homo habilis* (Latin for "handy man") was one of the first hominids to

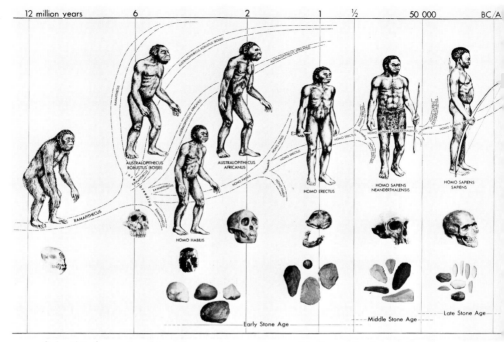

Early Stone Age • Middle Stone Age • Late Stone Age

*Scientists have pieced together a picture of humankind's origins in southern Africa.*

shape stones into crude tools for specific purposes, including cutting, scraping, and hammering tools for hunting and preparing food. The *Homo habilis* groups were more closely knit than those of the other early hominid, called *Australopithecus* by scientists. *Homo habilis* individuals shared food within their groups and traveled in bands for protection against animals.

By 1.5 million years ago, *Australopithecus* had died out and *Homo habilis* had evolved into *Homo erectus*, or "upright man." *Homo erectus* spread through eastern Africa. He was a nomadic hunter and gatherer, wandering in well-defined social and family groups. *Homo erectus* probably developed a crude language and certainly discovered the use of fire for cooking and warmth.

Modern humans, called *Homo sapiens*, or "thinking man," developed from *Homo erectus* around 100,000 years ago. Archaeologists (scientists who study the traces of bygone human cultures) call the period when *Homo sapiens* first roamed present-day Zimbabwe the Stone Age—a time when people began to use more complex stone tools than those used by their ancestors.

Fossil bones of early humans are very scarce. No ancient *Homo sapiens* have been found in Zimbabwe. The oldest such fossils discovered near Zimbabwe—the *Homo sapiens rhodesiansis*, found in Zambia—are only 30,000 years old. Archaeologists are still searching for human fossils in Zimbabwe and other eastern African nations. If unearthed, these fossils would help answer questions about the evolution and ways of life of early humans.

Although no bones have been uncovered, ancient humans left other traces in Zimbabwe. Flaked stone tools from rock shelters in Redcliff and Pomongwe in Zimbabwe are between 37,000 and 42,000 years old. Nearly 1,500 rock painting sites, dated around 7,000 years old, have been found in caves and on large granite boulders in the southwest savanna. The paintings show Stone Age humans hunting with bows and arrows and herding cattle. There are also figures of animals, birds, insects, and reptiles.

*Thousands of years ago, this digging stick or hammer belonged to a Stone Age Zimbabwean.*

*Today's few remaining Batwa are the descendants of the people who inhabited the region until about* A.D. *200.*

Archaeologists know that native peoples called Bushmen, or San people, lived in eastern Africa during the Stone Age. The Bushmen, whose descendants are found today in Namibia and Botswana's Kalahari Desert, were responsible for many of the Stone Age artifacts found in Zimbabwe. Some Bushmen groups were nomadic, moving around the region as the seasons changed; others established permanent settlements in favorable areas.

The Stone Age in Zimbabwe lasted until around the year A.D. 200, the start of the Iron Age. At the beginning of the Iron Age, peoples of the Bantu nation came from northern Africa and pushed many of the Bushmen southward; other Bushmen stayed in the region, however, and intermarriages between the Bantu and Bushmen were common. A few Bushmen retained their traditional culture in out-of-the-way parts of southwestern Zimbabwe. Their descendants are known as the Batwa people, but today they number only a few thousand.

The Bantu peoples introduced new methods of farming, cattle herding, and toolmaking. They brought the first pottery into the region and worked with metals by hammering or melting the ores into crude pots and tools. Their small farming communities were self-sufficient. Farmers grew grains such as millet and sorghum and tended goats, sheep, and cattle. By A.D. 1000, the Bantu people had settled throughout eastern Africa. They were the ancestors of the modern Shona- and Ndebele-speaking peoples.

## Great Zimbabwe

One of the most impressive relics of the early Bantu culture in Zimbabwe is a group of great stone buildings found around 29 miles (47 kilometers) southeast of Masvingo. Archaeologists believe the city was built by the native African kingdoms that existed in the area between A.D. 1100 and A.D. 1700, the most powerful of which was called the Rozwi kingdom. The tall stone structures are called Great Zimbabwe, the Zimbabwe Ruins, or the City of Stone, and many buildings still stand today.

The buildings of Great Zimbabwe are made of stones from the nearby granite-covered hills. There are three distinct sets of buildings. In the north is Hill Ruins (or Hill Complex), which stands around 328 feet (100 meters) above the rest of the ruins. The Hill Ruins contain many enclosures separated by freestanding walls. One enclosure contains a natural cave; a person who shouts there can be heard in the valley far below. Archaeologists believe that the complex may have been built around this cave, which was used as a religious shrine.

*Archaeological excavation of Great Zimbabwe began in the late 1800s.*

*An artist has portrayed the* dagas, *or mud huts, of the nobles of Great Zimbabwe.*

South of the Hill Ruins is the Elliptical Building. This structure, an irregular oval more than 1,804 feet (550 meters) around, is also called the Temple or the Great Enclosure. The outer wall is almost 32 feet (10 meters) high and more than 16 feet (5 meters) thick in some areas, making it one of the largest structures built before the 19th century in Africa south of the Sahara Desert. The Great Enclosure may have been built in the 1700s by the Rozwi kingdom, the successor to an earlier kingdom called the Monomotapa Dynasty. This enclosure probably housed the ruler's residence and court. Here the king would delegate authority to his various leaders and conduct important trade negotiations.

The Valley of Ruins, or Valley Complex, is between the Elliptical Building and Hill Ruins. It contains 10 ruins. Half of them were named after Europeans who explored Zimbabwe during the 19th century, including George Phillips, an English hunter and trader. These ruins probably housed the lesser officials and royal family members.

The term *zimbabwe* is derived from the Shona phrase *dzimba dza mabwe*, or "houses of stone," and is the source of the country's name. There are other ruins, or zimbabwes, around the country, such as the Khami Ruins outside of the city of Bulawayo or the Regina Ruins on the edge of Mbalabala. All of these ruins are believed to be evidence of the spread of the Great Zimbabwe culture. They probably housed the local chiefs of the different areas.

The history of Great Zimbabwe is still partly guesswork, but it is believed that the city was founded around A.D. 1100 by Bantu people who belonged to the large federation of tribal groups that shared the Shona language. By the 13th century, metalworking, stone carving, and weaving were very advanced in Great Zimbabwe.

By the 14th century, Great Zimbabwe's gold trading was flourishing, especially with Arab and Portuguese traders, who brought beads, textiles, and glassware in exchange for gold. The Shona-speaking peoples also traded slaves for goods, a common practice throughout most of Africa. It is believed that Great Zimbabwe was one of the earliest state systems and centers of international trade in southern Africa.

The city of stone became a ministate, filled with markets and warehouses. *Dagas*, or mud huts, were used for housing, for the royal palace, and for several religious shrines. It is believed that more than 10,000 people lived in the city.

The state system was very strong in Great Zimbabwe. The king was the absolute ruler. The society was based on cattle grazing and subsistence farming, which meant that the people of Great Zimbabwe grew just enough food to feed the city. The wealth of the state depended not on its own food production but on trade with various native African peoples and traders from other countries.

The culture of the ancient city is seen in the many artifacts that have been taken from the ruins at Great Zimbabwe. Some of the most famous are the Zimbabwe "birds," replicas of which can be seen on the flag, currency, and national coat of arms. The eight birds found at Great Zimbabwe actually resemble reptiles. They are 15 inches (36 centimeters) in height and are made of green soapstone,

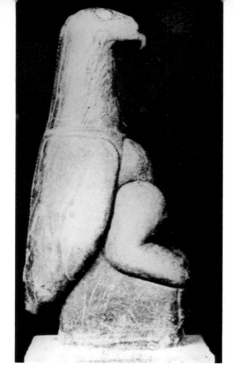

*Eight curious birdlike statues were found at Great Zimbabwe. The "Zimbabwe bird" is now a national symbol.*

a stone that is sturdy but easy to carve. It is believed that these figures represent the ancestral spirits of kings who once ruled Great Zimbabwe.

By the mid-1500s, Great Zimbabwe was abandoned. The resources that at one time made it an important state had been overused. The soil was no longer good for growing crops. The mines and grazing lands were depleted. But later cultures, impressed by the city's stone walls and shrines, raised new buildings, including the Great Enclosure.

From the 14th to the early 19th century, there was much fighting among various peoples in the region. Smaller groups sometimes tried to overpower the larger federations, such as Great Zimbabwe.

One large tribe that rose to power was the Shona-speaking Monomotapa tribe, also called Munhumutapa or Mwanamutapa. The Monomotapa moved into Great Zimbabwe, where the Portuguese contacted them in the late 15th century. At that time, the Monomotapa kingdom was at its peak. No one knows the relationship of the Monomotapa to the first rulers of Great Zimbabwe.

The Monomotapa lost power as they battled other peoples advancing from the north and south. The Shona-speaking Changamire were the strongest in Zimbabwe during the 17th through 19th centuries. They created the powerful Changamire Dynasty. By the mid-1600s, the Changamire had taken over several large territories, including Great Zimbabwe. They probably built additional buildings at Great Zimbabwe and at smaller zimbabwes around the area. Because of their warlike behavior, they were called the Rozwi, or "the destroyers."

During the 18th century, there were few European visitors. Most traders traveled along the outside boundaries of the frightful land that was ruled by the aggressive Changamire. But by the early 19th century, the Changamire Dynasty was in chaos. Fighting among the leaders of the group, a severe drought, and conflicts among the more than 100 independent Shona chiefdoms in the area combined to weaken the Changamire.

Instability in the Changamire Empire allowed other groups to take over. In the east was Mashonaland, where the Shona-speaking peoples ruled. Invaders from the south, a powerful group called the Ndebele, took over the southwest region, which came to be called Matabeleland.

## Explorers and Colonists

At the same time that the Ndebele settled in Matabeleland, Europeans again began to explore the region. For example, in 1824, Robert Moffet started a mission south of Zimbabwe in Bechuanaland, present-day Botswana. And David Livingstone, the famous Scottish missionary, visited and named the Victoria Falls on the Zambezi River around 1855.

*Scottish missionary-explorer David Livingstone discovered and named Victoria Falls.*

The ruins at Great Zimbabwe were explored by the Europeans during the mid-19th century. The first explorer to find the ruins was Adam Renders, a German-born American immigrant; Karl Mauch, a German geologist and the first to report gold in Zimbabwe, visited the ruins in 1871. His descriptions and maps of the ruins sent many European fortune hunters into the area, including some who mistakenly believed that the Zimbabwe Ruins were really King Solomon's lost gold mines. Most Europeans did not believe that the native black Africans were capable of developing such a sophisticated culture as Great Zimbabwe.

Europeans explored and hunted in the region, but few settled in Matabeleland or Mashonaland until one man decided to claim the region for Britain. He was Cecil Rhodes, an Englishman who became famous in South Africa as an explorer, financier, and politician.

Cecil John Rhodes was born in England in 1853. He came to South Africa because of poor health. There, he and his brother, Herbert, became wealthy in the diamond fields in the area now called Kimberly. He eventually became one of the owners of the diamond mines called De Beers Consolidated Mining, Ltd., one of today's largest diamond companies.

Rhodes became a millionaire, was elected to the South African parliament, and became one of the richest and most powerful men in South Africa. He was very patriotic, and his patriotism took the form of imperialism. That is, he believed that the British Empire had a right and a duty to expand into the "backward" regions of the earth. He particularly wanted Britain to gain control of as much African territory as possible; his dream was to see the British Union Jack flag flying from the Cape of Good Hope in South Africa to Cairo in Egypt. The first step was for the British in South Africa to move north into Matabeleland—into the area that is now Zimbabwe.

Rhodes obtained the land north of South Africa in a very aggressive manner. First, he sent Charles D. Rudd, his agent, to Matabeleland. Rudd was able to convince the chief of the Ndebele, Lobengula Khomalo, that Cecil Rhodes should be given limited mining rights in the land to the east, Mashonaland. Rudd offered money, goods, and rifles to Lobengula and his people. The Rudd Concession was signed by Lobengula in 1885. But Lobengula had been tricked: The concession was for *all* mining rights in Mashonaland and gave Rhodes complete control over the area.

Cecil Rhodes, one of the world's wealthiest men because of his diamond holdings, was a leader in the politics of South Africa and the guiding force behind white settlement in what is now Zimbabwe.

Rhodes formed the British South African Company (BSAC), later called the Charter Company. Although the British government would not fund the development of the country, in 1889 it granted a royal charter to the BSAC to explore, mine, and trade in the lands north of South Africa. Cecil Rhodes, who funded the company and intended to pay for the development of the land, was on his way to the north. In order to tame the wilderness and encourage other Europeans to settle in the northern regions, he formed the "Pioneer Column"—a group of men who made their way through Matabeleland and into the wilds of Mashonaland.

The Pioneer Column started from eastern Botswana at the end of June 1890. It cut a long swathe through the bush of the harsh savanna. Travel was difficult, especially with the dust of the dry savanna and the mud and high rivers of the rainy season. Most of the column walked for miles each day, carrying tools for chopping vegetation and building forts. The biggest problem was that the men did not know what to expect in a wilderness where animals, flash floods, and disease were common.

*A magazine cover illustration from 1890 shows Rhodes's Pioneer Column fording a river on its way to Mashonaland.*

*Rhodes wanted the British Union Jack to fly everywhere from Cairo to Cape Town.*

The column consisted of 212 men, mainly white South Africans, divided into three troops. They were called the Pioneer Corps. Five hundred members of the British South African Police were hired to guard the troops. Two hundred African mercenary soldiers from eastern Mozambique were brought along for additional protection. But there was little fighting with the Ndebele or Shona as the column cut its way through the wilderness. The African people did not fight with the troops because the natives did not believe that the Europeans would stay long in Mashonaland.

The Africans were wrong. As the column moved into Mashonaland, it opened numerous settlements along the way. Many forts were built as the column moved through the region, including Fort Tuli, at their starting point, and Fort Victoria, now called Masvingo. In three months, the Europeans were settled in Mashonaland. Their influence was explosive. The Europeans appeared to colonize the land overnight, especially when compared to the long history of the native peoples before the arrival of the settlers.

Rhodes promised each man in the Pioneer Corps a 3,000-acre piece of land and up to 15 gold claims in the new territory. On September 12, 1890, at the site of Fort Salisbury (now Harare, the capital of Zimbabwe), Mashonaland was claimed for the British. The column disbanded, and most of its members left to search for gold.

The era of European influence began: British rule had come to Mash-onaland, and Cecil Rhodes had realized his dream of expanding the British Empire. In 1891, Great Britain formally declared Rhodesia a British protectorate—that is, a region under British "protection" in which other nations could not make claims or settle colonists.

Word of the settlements spread, and the number of European settlers increased. The early years were difficult. Goods such as food, building materials, cloth, and some livestock could be brought in only along the Pioneer Column route. Heavy rains brought more hardships, swelling rivers and making the Pioneer Column route impassable. It often took months for food and equipment to be sent to the new settlements.

In a few short years, however, new roads were built. The settlers tamed the land. They developed farming and mining communities, especially in the eastern highlands. Still under the contract of the Charter Company, the settlers named their new land "Rhodesia," in honor of Cecil Rhodes. But there was growing trouble with the native people, who were beginning to resent the invasion of their lands by the white Europeans.

The Ndebele were the first to rise up against the Europeans, in 1893. Much of the Ndebele economy was based on raiding other African groups, especially the Shona. The Europeans had taken the

*Nbedele warriors resisted the British with stolen muskets as well as native spears.*

Shona into their communities, using the natives for work around the farms and mines. This protection prevented the Ndebele from attacking the Shona. In retaliation, the Ndebele clashed with the Europeans—and lost.

By 1896, Europeans occupied much of Mashonaland and central Matabeleland. With each new settlement, the Ndebele became more angry with the Charter Company. In addition, many of the Shona protested being forced to work on European farms and were angry that cattle were seized from their land.

There were other problems. Many of the black Africans were forced off their land and were segregated from the whites. Jobs and salaries for blacks were determined by the white settlers. Whites decided where the black people would live—even whom they would marry.

At the same time, *rinderpest,* a cattle disease, broke out. Thousands of cattle had to be shot. Crop-devouring insects called locusts brought the threat of famine. These problems added to the anger of the Ndebele and Shona peoples. In March 1896, the Ndebele began to attack again, killing African policemen and white Europeans. By the end of March, almost every black African kingdom in Rhodesia was in revolt—trying to break the power of the Charter Company.

The Ndebele were soon joined by several of the Shona groups from the north and central parts of Rhodesia. But the Europeans had the advantage. They were assisted by additional European fighting forces from South Africa; they had better firearms; they constructed large, impenetrable *laagers,* or "army encampments," around certain towns; and they believed that they had a moral duty to conquer and tame the country and its black African people.

The war was costly in terms of lives and money. Cecil Rhodes decided to end it. In August 1896, he began his first *indaba,* or "meeting," with black African leaders in the south. In December, the Ndebele surrendered, followed by the Shona in January 1897.

*Blacks labored to build the railroads that Rhodes needed to open new trade routes.*

After the war of 1896, the officials of the Charter Company divided Rhodesia into Northern Rhodesia (today's Zambia) and Southern Rhodesia (today's Zimbabwe). Cecil Rhodes may be the only person in history to have two countries named after him.

Southern Rhodesia grew rapidly. The Charter Company had learned a valuable lesson, and it reorganized its administration to cope with the problems of a growing nation. Telegraph lines were extended from north to south, and the first railroads were built from the south into the town of Bulawayo. Other railroad lines were built from Beira, Mozambique, to Southern Rhodesia, opening important trade lines to and from the Indian Ocean. Mining increased, especially of gold and coal. Farming methods and techniques were improved, allowing for the extensive production of corn, tobacco, tea, and cotton.

By 1898, more than 13,000 Europeans lived in Southern Rhodesia. But the country had become a country divided on the basis of color: The white Europeans continued to dominate the larger population of blacks. Whites had the best land for farming and the best schools. Although blacks had voting privileges, the requirements for voting were based on level of education and income. Because few blacks were allowed to be educated and even fewer had money, few of them could vote.

White rule did bring prosperity and peace to the country. Tribal wars were halted. Medical care increased, and farming and cattle raising became profitable businesses. As the economy of the country rose, so did the standard of living for everyone in Southern Rhodesia.

Cecil Rhodes died in 1902 and was buried at Matopos Hills. With his death, the white settlers of Southern Rhodesia became unhappy with the rule of the Charter Company. The settlers wanted to be governed by the white people in their own country, not by a board of directors in England.

The British government finally intervened. It gave the people of the Rhodesias a choice: Join the Union of South Africa or become a British colony under a new constitution. Some of the property owners wanted to join South Africa; others wanted to become a British colony.

In 1923, the whites voted, and Cecil Rhodes's Charter Company came to an end. Southern Rhodesia became a self-governing British colony, ruled mainly by an elected parliament, while Northern Rhodesia remained a British protectorate. The British government retained various powers over Southern Rhodesia, including regulating the rights of the black African majority.

The next 30 years brought great prosperity to the country. Towns grew, as did the economy of Southern Rhodesia. Northern Rhodesia also prospered, especially through the mining of huge copper deposits. In particular, as the demand for minerals and metals grew during World War II, mines and industries within both countries benefited.

*Copper mine employees in 1958 worked under a police guard as unrest grew among the black population.*

By 1952, Southern Rhodesia, Northern Rhodesia, and Nyasaland (a British protectorate to the north that is now the nation of Malawi) agreed to form a federation, or united government. They hoped that by sharing each other's resources and technology, they would attract foreign investments and stimulate the economic growth of all three nations.

The Federation of Rhodesia and Nyasaland was the result of the union of the three countries in 1953. The federation government included a parliament, which consisted of members from all three nations. The majority of the members were white Europeans.

The federation was still under the thumb of Great Britain because the British government had special veto powers. For example, in 1957 the British government was called on to veto a voting law that discriminated against the black Africans. The British government could have vetoed the legislation but chose to let it stand.

During the next ten years, the federation brought economic prosperity to its member nations. Its economy was based largely on the copper exports of Northern Rhodesia, which sold at record high prices around the world in the mid-1950s. Southern Rhodesia received most of the benefits from the union of the nations. The Kariba Dam was built for hydroelectric power; the country contained the federal capital, Salisbury (now Harare); industries grew, as did railroad lines; and it received the largest share of money, greatly increasing its economic base.

Though the economy of the three countries increased, there was discrimination against the black African majority. In an era when blacks in many African colonies were demanding participation in government or even independence, Rhodesia's black majority was becoming aware of its lack of political power—and of its potential strength. Violence swept the African continent in the 1950s as black Africans sought to share or seize power from whites who had withheld it for decades.

In 1959, black Africans rioted in Nyasaland and Northern Rhodesia. The British government stepped in, setting up the Monckton Commission to determine whether the constitution of the federation should be changed. The commission found that there was great opposition to the federation from black Africans, especially those who lived in Nyasaland and Northern Rhodesia. Britain's only recommendation was for both nations to secede from the federation. On December 31, 1963, Northern Rhodesia and Nyasaland left the federation. In 1964, these countries became the independent states of Zambia and Malawi, governed by their black majorities.

Southern Rhodesia changed its name back to Rhodesia and remained a British colony. The white Rhodesian minority held all the political power, but the black majority was not prepared to let white rule continue.

*Election fever swept Rhodesia in 1979 as the black majority prepared to elect a leader. Abel Muzorewa of the United African National Council was one of the candidates for prime minister.*

# The Fight for Majority Rule

In 1963, after the Federation of Rhodesia and Nyasaland was dissolved, Southern Rhodesia dropped the "Southern" from its name. Along with the change in name came the desire to be independent of British supervision. The whites of the colony voted to break away from Britain, but Britain did not agree because the black majority in Rhodesia still had no political rights.

At the same time, nationalism—the belief that each people should be permitted to govern itself—was growing among African blacks. By 1964, all of Britain's former African colonies were independent and ruled by majority vote—except Rhodesia. Some Rhodesian blacks formed nationalist organizations to work for African rights. The National Democratic party (NDP) was founded in 1960 by a group of black African politicians and nationalists who called for a gradual change to black majority rule in Southern Rhodesia. The increase in the number of groups like the NDP helped Britain to decide that Rhodesia should be ruled by its black majority.

But the whites who had settled Rhodesia had other ideas. They felt that Rhodesia was their country, that its successes were based on what whites had accomplished. Although blacks outnumbered

*Joshua Nkomo (center) was the leader of the ZAPU party.*

whites 30 to 1, whites controlled most of the colony's money and its government, and they saw no reason to give up that control.

While the British government tried to decide the fate of Rhodesia, the white Rhodesian government was in conflict. Winston Field, the seventh prime minister of Rhodesia, was under attack both from various black nationalist groups and from his own political party, the white Rhodesian Front (RF), because of his reluctance to push for independence from Britain. The RF believed that Rhodesia's government should not have to answer to either Great Britain or the black population of Rhodesia. In April 1964, a new leader emerged in the RF and took over from Prime Minister Field. He was Ian Smith, born in Rhodesia's Selukwe district, and he pledged to secure Rhodesia's independence from Britain and to maintain white minority rule.

Ian Smith's white government was determined to rule Rhodesia. The ancestors of these whites had settled the land after much hardship. Many RF members had been born in the colony, and they considered themselves true Rhodesians, not Europeans. They had a plan for Rhodesia: to guarantee its economic future by building more schools and educating more skilled laborers. With a better-educated labor force, agricultural and mining practices would make Rhodesia economically secure.

Ian Smith's plans included most of the white Rhodesians, but the black majority was not so fortunate. A few days after arriving in office, Smith arrested several black nationalists, including Joshua Nkomo, the leader of ZAPU (Zimbabwe African People's Union,

*Prime Minister Ian Smith led the white movement to retain power.*

*Under Smith's government, white police (left) shadowed Nkomo (center) and other black nationalists.*

formerly part of the NDP), an organization made up mostly of Nde-bele who favored black majority rule. Smith also tried to negotiate with the British government for the freedom of Rhodesia. Many talks were held in England and Rhodesia, but the two countries remained in a deadlock.

In October 1965, Smith broke off relations with the British government. He was no longer concerned about what Britain had to say. On November 11, he signed the Unilateral Declaration of In-

*In 1965, Smith signed a declaration that made Rhodesia a white-ruled nation.*

dependence (UDI) and announced Rhodesia's independence. For the second time in less than 200 years, a colony had declared its independence from Britain illegally, or without British consent. (The first was the United States.)

Britain and the world retaliated against Smith's government. Britain refused to recognize Rhodesia as an independent state. It placed economic sanctions, or penalties, on Rhodesia; these included halting British purchases of Rhodesian sugar and tobacco and the refusal of British banks to lend money to Rhodesia. In addition, members of the United Nations declared sanctions on the Smith government, demanding that all member countries of the United Nations break off trade with Rhodesia.

Rhodesia survived most of the sanctions. The government learned to be more careful with its funds, and money was invested at home. Rhodesian farmers learned to improve their methods of growing crops. For example, the quality and production of tobacco, corn, wheat, sugar, and other crops were improved. Cotton farms increased in number and production, creating jobs and materials for Rhodesia's expanding textile industry.

Rhodesia's mineral wealth helped. Metal ore and mineral mines supplied raw materials to industry within its own borders. The country's vast reserves included copper, lithium, coal, and chrome. Hydropower from large dams, such as the one at Lake Kariba, was used to run the many mines and industries. Rhodesia seemed well on the way toward achieving Smith's goal of self-sufficiency.

Some countries did not participate in the sanctions against Rhodesia. Supplies were regularly delivered from the Republic of South Africa and the Portuguese colonies Angola and Mozambique. Rhodesia exported many raw materials to bordering countries that were sympathetic to the Rhodesian cause, including corn to South Africa. Zambia depended on Rhodesia for food, coal, railway lines, and hydroelectric power from the Kariba Dam.

Economic sanctions imposed by most of the world were not the only obstacle the white Rhodesian government had to overcome. Smith's unilateral declaration of independence also brought about major problems with the black majority because it did not include

*Economic sanctions forced Rhodesia to rely on its own thriving industries.*

*In 1962, a veteran of the 1890s rebellions against the British gave Nkomo (left) a ceremonial ax as a symbol of resistance.*

voting rights for the black Rhodesian peoples. Black political and nationalist groups gained strength. Chief among them were Nkomo's ZAPU and the Shona-dominated ZANU (Zimbabwe African National Union). Some of the most influential black nationalist leaders had been educated in Great Britain or the United States. With education had come an awareness of black liberation movements in other parts of Africa and increased resentment at white domination.

Fighting between black nationalists and the white government began in Chinhoyi on April 28, 1966. The first act of the Rhodesian civil war occurred when ZANU's military wing, ZANLA (Zimbabwe African National Liberation Army), sent seven black guerrillas to attack strategic targets in the heart of a major white farming community. The seven were killed, outnumbered by the white forces.

The black guerrillas had to be trained in other countries, because people who opposed Smith's government were often arrested by Rhodesia's strong police force. Rhodesia's army and police forces were among the best trained in Africa and were composed of white and black men loyal to Smith's government.

After the first few skirmishes, the two major black political groups, ZAPU and ZANU, decided to seek help from outside Rhodesia in order to increase their chances of winning battles against the government forces. ZAPU's military wing, ZIPRA (Zimbabwe People's

Revolutionary Army), under the leadership of Joshua Nkomo and commanded by Lieutenant General Lookout Masuku, trained in Zambia. ZANU's military wing, ZANLA, with Robert Mugabe as its leader, operated in Mozambique, especially after Mozambique declared independence from Portuguese rule in 1975. ZAPU and ZANU leaders helped recruit and train black volunteers to fight against the Rhodesian government forces. ZANLA was supplied and trained mainly by the Chinese; the Soviets contributed arms and training to ZIPRA guerrilla forces.

ZANLA guerrillas eventually found a way to enter Rhodesia without raising the suspicions of the government forces. Guerrillas entered villages in teams of 20 or more. In all-night meetings called *pungwes*, they lectured the villagers about the need for majority rule. Because they spoke the same language and shared the same cultural traditions, Shona villagers cooperated with the ZANLA guerrillas.

*A ZANU publication from the 1970s showed men and women guerrillas fighting side by side.*

Both ZANU and ZAPU were fighting for the same cause—the freedom of Rhodesia from the rule of the white minority. But neither guerrilla army was willing to cooperate with the other. The two major native African groups in Rhodesia, the Ndebele and the Shona, had fought each other for centuries. Though both were opposed to white rule, political and cultural differences continued to keep them at odds with each other. ZAPU, the Ndebele group, and ZANU, the Shona group, fought with each other as well as with the Smith regime.

As the fighting continued in his country, Ian Smith tried to negotiate an acceptable constitution with the British government in order to end the economic sanctions. The first discussions, held aboard the British cruiser *Tiger* and called the "*Tiger* talks," took place between Smith and British prime minister Harold Wilson about five months after the UDI. The negotiations failed, and economic sanctions against Rhodesia continued.

A second discussion, the "*Fearless* talks," began in October 1968. Again, Wilson and Smith, this time aboard the warship *Fearless*, could not agree on a reasonable constitution. Smith believed that Britain was asking for too much control over the Rhodesian government.

Segregation of whites and blacks in Rhodesia increased in 1969. Smith's government announced the Land Tenure Act, dividing the country into a patchwork of racially segregated lands. The 6 million black Africans were given a few acres called tribal trust lands—overcrowded lands that had a great amount of soil erosion. The 250,000 whites were given the best territory, mainly in the High Veld.

Smith's government made another major declaration in 1970: Rhodesia was now the Republic of Rhodesia. Smith remained prime minister and head of government, and Clifford Dupont became the president, or formal head of state. The whites continued to rule the

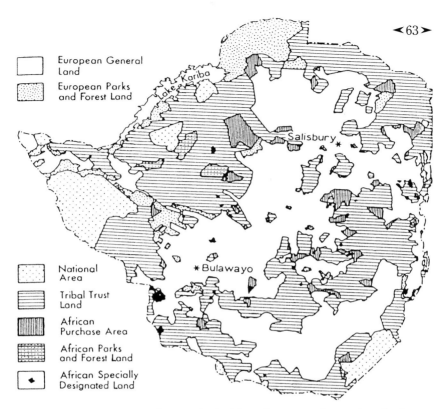

European General
Land

European Parks
and Forest Land

National
Area

Tribal Trust
Land

African
Purchase Area

African Parks
and Forest Land

African Specially
Designated Land

Lake Kariba

Salisbury

*Bulawayo

*With the Land Tenure Act of 1969, the Smith regime created a patchwork of racial segregation. The High Veld and other choice territories went to the whites.*

country; 50 members of Smith's party, the RF, were elected to the parliament.

The Smith government also declared a small victory against economic sanctions in 1971: The U.S. Congress passed the Byrd Amendment, which allowed the United States to import chrome from Rhodesia. The United States was criticized by most of the world because the act defied UN sanctions against Rhodesia. The act was repealed by U.S. president Jimmy Carter in 1978. After 1978, Rhodesia did not suffer because of the loss of money from the United States, but it did suffer from the loss of moral support.

The Republic of Rhodesia was brought back into the world spotlight in 1972. Britain was again trying to offer alternatives to the Rhodesian government. It called for a new constitution in a major proposal called the Anglo-Rhodesian Settlement. The proposal said that black representation in parliament was to increase immediately, that the government must work on an end to racial discrimination, that the cases of all political prisoners in Rhodesian jails would be reviewed, and that a plan would be developed to bring about majority rule. But the new proposal did not eliminate existing discriminatory laws, and it appeared that black majority rule would not come about for many decades. Furthermore, it left Smith's government in control.

The black nationalists responded to the proposal by forming the African National Council (ANC). Led by Abel Tendekayi Muzorewa and Canaan Banana, both religious ministers with no political background, the ANC opposed the proposal. The group grew rapidly and encouraged protests against the proposal in black communities. Soon the two major black nationalist parties, ZAPU and ZANU, along with a smaller group called FROLIZI (Front for the Liberation of Zimbabwe), came together under the banner of the ANC to fight the British proposal.

In 1972, the 24-member Pearce Commission, under the leadership of Lord Edward Pearce, was formed to test the acceptability of the proposal to the Rhodesian people. Through interviews, the commission members hoped to learn the Rhodesians' reaction to the ideas in the Anglo-Rhodesian Settlement. The commission found that most of the white Rhodesians approved of the proposal, but almost all of the black Rhodesians rejected it, mainly because of the influence of the ANC. Britain then abandoned the proposal, knowing that the majority of Rhodesians would not accept it.

The activities of the Pearce Commission brought about an increase in black Rhodesian nationalism, as seen in the formation of

*(continued on p. 73)*

# SCENES OF
# ZIMBABWE

◄ *Kariba Dam, built across the Zambezi River in the 1950s, produces electricity for both Zimbabwe and its neighbor Zambia.*

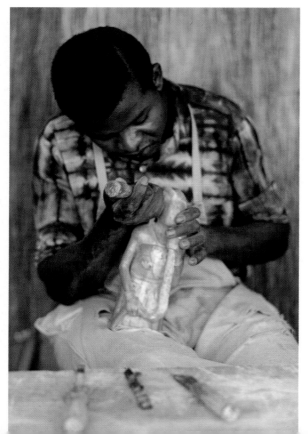

◄ *A craftsman carves a figurine from soapstone. The same kind of stone was used by the carvers who lived in Great Zimbabwe to produce the "Zimbabwe birds" and other relics and artifacts.*

◄ *Some teachers take their classrooms out into the cornfields to reach the children of farming families.*

⋎ *A Ndebele home in Harare is decorated with traditional painted geometric designs and symbols.*

◄ *A member of the colorful family of birds called rollers surveys the savanna from his vantage point on a bush. Rollers are named for their acrobatic courtship flights, which include rolls, loops, and other aerial maneuvers.*

˅ *Zebras visit a water hole in one of many wildlife preserves.*

▲ *This kudu is safe from hunters at Hwange National Park.*

▼ *Safari trophies are now taken with cameras, not rifles.*

➤ *The sun sets over Bulawayo. Once the headquarters of the Ndebele chief Lobengula, it is now Zimbabwe's second largest city.*

⋎ *The Matopos Hills, near Harare, are one of the country's best-known scenic attractions.*

∨ *In the spring, avenues of flowering trees carpet the pavements with fallen blooms.*

▲ *The Elliptical Building at Great Zimbabwe is more than 1,804 feet (550 meters)
around and 32 feet (10 meters) high. It is one of the largest structures to be
built before the 19th century in all of Africa south of the Sahara Desert.* Inset:
*Cone-shaped towers of stone are scattered throughout the ruins; their purpose
is unknown.*

(continued from p. 64)

the ANC. Mass demonstrations were held in cities. Violence grew at an alarming rate; police arrested many demonstrators and killed at least a dozen of them. Guerrilla action increased, including attacks on and killings of soldiers, policemen, and white farmers.

In 1974, with the civil war still taking its toll on both blacks and whites, Smith's government recognized the need to protect white citizens from black nationalist guerrillas. Smith started the "protected villages" campaign, concentrating small villages of black farmers into areas surrounded by chain-link fences and patrolled by soldiers. This plan was designed to keep whites safe in the country and to attract European immigrants, but it also served to cut off communication between the black nationalist guerrillas and the villages.

As time passed, Smith realized that he could not stamp out black nationalism. In addition, he felt that Rhodesia needed the approval and recognition of other nations. The results of the Pearce Commission influenced him, and both U.S. secretary of state Henry Kissinger and Prime Minister John Vorster of South Africa urged him to consider majority rule. In 1976, he met with leaders of the guerrilla movements. But while Smith, the Rhodesian government, and black leaders argued over how to make the transition to majority rule, the fighting between black nationalists and government forces continued in Rhodesia.

Negotiations for the transition to majority rule proceeded slowly. But in 1978, Smith and three black nationalists, Ndabaningi Sithole, J. S. Chirau, and Bishop Abel Tendekayi Muzorewa—called the Salisbury Four—signed an agreement that was supposed to begin the transition to majority rule.

This gesture of reconciliation did little to stop the violence in the country. Many blacks wanted Smith out immediately, and many whites resented Smith's move toward majority rule. Black and white civilians were killed in the crossfire between government troops and

*South African prime minister John Vorster (right) was an early supporter of Smith (left).*

guerrillas. The government conducted raids into Mozambique and Zambia, killing hundreds of Rhodesian guerrillas who lived in camps there. Joshua Nkomo's ZAPU claimed responsibility for shooting down an Air Rhodesian airliner, saying the civilians aboard were really on a military mission. Smith reacted by enforcing martial law and strict curfews on trouble spots. By late 1978, half of Rhodesia was under martial law, and many nationalists had been arrested and jailed.

In an effort to bring about a peaceful transition to majority rule, the Rhodesian government made an agreement with Bishop Muzorewa in 1979. He was to become prime minister of the country,

*Rhodesian housewives practiced their marksmanship on targets painted with figures of black guerrillas.*

*Black residents of the "protected village" in the background lined up to vote in the 1979 elections.*

which would be renamed Zimbabwe-Rhodesia. But Joshua Nkomo and Robert Mugabe protested that their political parties must be included in the government or ZAPU and ZANU guerrillas would continue fighting. This threat killed the idea of forming Zimbabwe-Rhodesia.

With British help, a new Rhodesian constitution was written, calling for parliamentary elections in early 1979—with blacks free to vote. Smith's government, tired of the long civil war, agreed to let the elections take place. When they were held, blacks were elected to 80 percent of the parliamentary seats. (The remaining 20 percent were reserved for whites under the constitution.) Most of these seats went to Robert Mugabe's ZANU party. Mugabe had become the most powerful man in the country.

When he signed Zimbabwe's new constitution in London in 1979, Mugabe gave Zimbabwe a fresh start. On April 18, 1980, Rhodesia was declared legally and unquestionably independent. It became the Republic of Zimbabwe, with Robert Mugabe, the leader of ZANU, as prime minister.

## Troubles of a New Nation

The civil war had finally ended. The 15-year struggle had cost millions of dollars and more than 27,000 lives. Some of the victims were white farmers and politicians; some were armed black guerril-

*A captured nationalist guerrilla stands amid the bodies of 17 other fighters and 2 civilians slain in a clash in 1976.*

las; others were blacks and whites of the government army and police forces. But most were bystanders, not fighters, black or white citizens from rural areas who were caught in the crossfire between black nationalist guerrillas and government troops and police.

The elections had given some support to Joshua Nkomo, the leader of ZAPU, who became the minister of home affairs. The office of president, which had little real power, was given to Canaan Banana of ZANU. After the elections, it appeared that the new government could accommodate both races and all political parties. ZAPU, ZANU, and whites were to rule the country in peace—at least for a while.

In 1982, after a dispute with Mugabe, Nkomo left the government; some say Mugabe threatened to kill him if he remained in office. Former ZAPU guerrillas then began a campaign of terror against whites, kidnapping tourists and killing farmers—any tactic to cause trouble for the ruling ZANU party. In 1985, during national elections in which Nkomo and Muzorewa ran against Mugabe, many ZAPU and ZANU candidates who were running for various offices were murdered. Mugabe won another five-year term, but the victory created renewed hostility between the two political parties. In 1986, leaders of ZANU and ZAPU tried to merge the two groups into a united party, but the union broke down less than a year later. Since the leaders could not agree to cooperate, violence broke out again in Matabeleland, the Ndebele homeland, and it was blamed on ZAPU, the Shona party. Mugabe's government cracked down on ZAPU, arresting many party leaders. Finally, in 1989, ZANU and ZAPU once again arranged a merger, and this time the union was strong enough to last.

In the late 1980s, Mugabe also campaigned against the remaining whites of the government. He claimed that the 1979 constitution contained several provisions that favored the whites, such as the reservation of 20 of the 100 seats in the House of Assembly and 10 of the 40 Senate seats for the whites—a disproportionate number, as the whites represent only 2 percent of the population. In 1987, the government abolished the reserved seats. When elections were held to fill the 30 vacancies, 15 whites and 15 blacks were elected; all were members of ZANU. Another change in the constitution, also in 1987, combined the posts of president and prime minister into one position called executive president. Canaan Banana quietly resigned from the presidency, and Mugabe became Zimbabwe's first executive president.

Since coming to power, Mugabe's government has enacted several comprehensive economic reform plans for Zimbabwe. In the years immediately following independence in 1980, ideas for reform

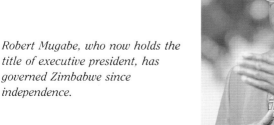

*Robert Mugabe, who now holds the title of executive president, has governed Zimbabwe since independence.*

were reflected in a socialist Five-Year Plan. That plan promoted agriculture, the development of mineral resources, and an increase in manufacturing. It aimed to revolutionize and upgrade Zimbabwe's industries and better train the labor force. Schools were built to educate scientists and engineers and to conduct research into better methods of farming and generating energy.

The Five-Year Plan urged that private enterprise be eliminated and that factories and farming communities be operated as state-run cooperatives. This arrangement, however, did not last long. Government spending and subsidies ballooned, leading to budget deficits and high inflation. When the Soviet Union collapsed at the end of the 1980s and a newly democratic South Africa came into being in 1994, offering itself as a powerful trading partner, the Zimbabwe government realized that the international economic climate was changing. By this time the government had begun to omit references to Marxism from its platform.

In the same period, Zimbabwe entered a prolonged drought, lasting through the mid-1990s. The drought years devastated agricultural output, brought famine to the land, and further damaged the country's growth and finances. Mugabe appealed to the world for help. In exchange for loans from the International Monetary Fund and the World Bank, Zimbabwe had to pledge to reduce spending and inflation and to privatize many large industries that were still government owned.

Under these pressures Mugabe, who was solidly re-elected in 1996, has modified his socialist beliefs to accept free enterprise and competition as essential to Zimbabwe's success. Private businesses now exist side-by-side with state-owned media and industries. The press is still partially state-controlled, however, and the executive branch often overshadows the legislative and judicial branches.

The government's current challenges include repaying Zimbabwe's debts and negotiating the troubled waters of international

*At a ceremony in Salisbury, Britain's Prince Charles (far left) saluted as the Union Jack was lowered for the last time in April 1980.*

trade. At home, the government hopes to keep spending under control, encourage production in factories, farms, and mines, and initiate bold new projects in tourism. These are complicated tasks. Many critics wonder where the funding will be found to pay for the new international airport in Harare and the proposed digital telecommunications system at a time when currency exchange rates are poor and debts are high. Moreover, since AIDS prevention has been discussed only marginally in public, some wonder whether the government can adequately confront the challenge of keeping the population healthy. Despite these problems, many think that the freedom from ongoing civil war gives Zimbabwe its best prospects since independence.

*Zimbabwe's black population is divided between the rival Shona and Ndebele, but the two cultures are very similar. The spirit medium in this old photo could belong to either.*

# People and Culture

Zimbabwe has a population of 11,300,000. It is a multiracial country. About 87 percent of its people are black Africans; the other 13 percent are Europeans (mainly of British, Dutch, or German descent), Asians, and people of mixed blood. Although black Africans are considered one racial group, they are from a multitude of different ethnic groups, with different cultures and customs.

The easiest way to classify the various black African peoples is by language. More than 800 languages are spoken in Africa, and more than 2,000 linguistic groups, or clans, have their own versions of these languages, which are called dialects.

In Zimbabwe, there are three major languages and dozens of dialects. The major languages are Shona, Ndebele, and English. English is the official language, but 80 percent of the black Zimbabweans speak languages or dialects that belong to the Shona family of languages. Chishona is the most widespread of the Shona languages. The principal Ndebele language is Sindebele, which is related to the language of the Zulu tribes of South Africa. Some languages in Zimbabwe are spoken by millions of people; others are confined to a few hundred people, perhaps to a single isolated community. Many of the older languages have become extinct. The oldest surviving language is Batwa, which is spoken by the remnants of the country's original Bushmen people.

Traditionally, the Shona peoples have been concentrated in the eastern part of Zimbabwe, and the Ndebele in the southwestern part. The Shona are divided into six groups, depending on the province in which they live: the Zezuru, the Korekore, the Manyika, the Ndau, the Kalanga (although most of this group has been absorbed by the Ndebele), and the Karanga (whose ancestors are thought to have made much of the pottery found at Great Zimbabwe). The name Shona is a European distortion of Maswina, which is what these peoples call themselves. The Ndebele are probably related to the Zulu kingdom of South Africa.

The Shona and Ndebele are direct descendants of the Bantu nation. A thousand years or more ago, the Bantu migrated into eastern Africa from the north. They were divided into two main groups of tribes: the Shona-speaking (called Mashona by the Europeans) and Ndebele-speaking (called Matabele).

When European influence began in Rhodesia in the late 1800s, most of the Shona and Ndebele people held on to their customs and culture. Unlike some colonial powers, the British settlers did not eject the natives from the country. Many blacks continued to live as they had before the British arrived; thus, many of the ancient customs of the Shona and Ndebele survived.

One such custom of the Shona and the Ndebele throughout the centuries has been storytelling—recounting myths, legends, folktales, puzzles, poetry, proverbs, and songs. Much of what is known today about the cultures and histories of the Shona and Ndebele comes from stories that were told in villages from generation to generation. Certain people in each tribe were taught stories of the village by their parents or grandparents. The next generation would then learn traditional customs, such as when to plant crops, from the storyteller. The stories were carefully memorized, as were the gestures of the narrator. The storytellers were able to preserve highly accurate oral records over long periods of time.

Many customs of the Shona and Ndebele are based on religious beliefs. For example, the Shona have always believed in the existence of life after death. Men and women, even after death, are expected to protect their living descendants. When a person dies, the Shona stage an elaborate ceremony to convert the dead into an ancestor, or *midzimu*—a spirit believed to be able to cure every ill, take care of the villages and farms, and predict the future. The midzimu has no material form, but people often call upon the midzimu of an ancestor for advice.

A year after the ancestor has died, the Shona have another ceremony to persuade the midzimu to protect the village. The Shona believe that the ancestor takes possession of the body of one of its descendants in order to share daily life. The possessed descendant becomes a medium. The Shona believe that the midzimu gives the medium special and important skills, such as the ability to cure illness or to carve in stone. The most important spirits are of past Shona chiefs, known as *mhondoro*, or lion spirits. Senior members of the community are usually the mediums of Shona chiefs.

*A medium is about to be possessed by a* midzimu, *or ancestral spirit.*

Mediums have played an important part in the Shona peoples' history. During the British settlement of Rhodesia, spirit mediums from various communities were called upon to lead the rebellion against the settlers. During the 15-year civil war, black nationalists often requested support from mediums. The mediums were invited to attend political meetings and asked to use their powers to help the nationalists defeat the Smith forces. Today mediums live ordinary lives within their communities but still are called upon to help grow crops or heal the sick.

Many Ndebele customs also have survived through the centuries. As with the Shona, many Ndebele customs are concerned with the spirit world. The Ndebele believe that certain people are in touch with particular spirits. For example, a person who has a beautiful garden is in harmony with the spirit in charge of growing crops.

Zimbabweans of European descent have many British customs, which are followed in the larger cities, where the white population is greatest. These customs include afternoon tea (a light meal eaten in the late afternoon) and the sports of cricket and polo.

Economic differences linger between whites and most of the black Zimbabweans, although the races are equal in the eyes of the Zimbabwean government. There are more wealthy blacks than ever before, but whites retain much of the money, especially those who

*Lawn bowling is a sport inherited from the British.*

*Harare, like the country's other large cities, has a mixture of races and cultures.*

live in the larger cities or own big farms. The government, especially in its socialist phase, has tried to distribute the wealth through social reforms, but the property rights of those who own land or businesses are protected by the constitution.

Most Zimbabweans in the cities earn their living as businessmen or politicians. Others, such as waiters and haircutters, work in the service professions. Almost all city dwellers rent apartments. Around the cities, people live in simple homes in the suburbs; most suburban houses have large gardens in their backyards. At one time, the suburbs were racially segregated. Since independence, however, neighborhoods are open to both blacks and whites.

People in the cities dress in the latest fashions, as many of the shops are supplied by the United States and European countries. Businessmen wear suits; businesswomen wear dresses or suits. Casual wear often includes a T-shirt. Some British men still dress in the traditional khaki shorts, shirts with epaulets, and knee socks— a style that was popular with the early European settlers. Some black Africans in the cities dress in the traditional turbanlike headdresses and brightly colored flowing shirts or robes of the Ndebele or Shona.

Food is easier to come by in the city than in the savanna. Most of the roads, railways, and airports are located in the cities, making it easy for food to be quickly and conveniently moved from city to city. For example, fresh fish is readily available throughout the country, transported to major cities by rail and road from fisheries such as those at Lake Kariba.

# Family Life

Family life in the city is much like that in Western nations. Women may choose to work at home or outside. Children must go to school until they are 15 years old. Students often attend colleges, either in Zimbabwe or another country. Watching sports events is a favorite pastime of many families in the city, as is visiting national parks or recreational areas.

City families are usually smaller than those in the back-country savanna. Most young people marry after a courtship, but there are also some families that follow the centuries-old African custom of marriage arranged by the father. Traditionally, Shona and Ndebele marriages were arranged by the bride's father, who chose a husband for his daughter. The groom provided a *lobola*, or "bride price"— usually a gift of cattle, goats, or sheep given to the father in token exchange for the bride. If the wife did not bear a child, the husband could give up the wife and demand the return of his lobola. Or the husband could have the bride's sister as a second wife; in fact, polygamy, or marriage to more than one wife, was common. Women had few or no independent rights; a woman was expected to be under the control first of her father and then of her husband.

Today black Zimbabwean women have much greater control over their lives. Women played a great role in the struggle for in-

The country's wealthiest people, mostly whites, enjoy Western-style luxuries.

*The poorest members of the rural population live much as their ancestors did a hundred years ago.*

dependence, often fighting in the guerrilla bands. The new government has passed many laws involving women's rights. For example, the Legal Age of Majority Act gives every man and woman over the age of 18 adult status. As an adult, a Zimbabwean woman can choose a career—and can also make her own decisions about marriage. The Sex Disqualification Act of 1980 gave women the right to hold public office and to participate in public functions.

In the back-country savanna and highlands, most Zimbabweans earn their living from the land. The savanna in the southwest and west supplies ample grazing grounds for livestock, and the fertile highlands are good for crops such as tea, tobacco, and cotton.

Most homes in the back country are mud huts. Other homes, especially around mining towns, are made of cement or brick. There are some modern houses in the back country, especially on the larger farms. Smaller savanna villages have few buildings besides houses; some of the larger towns, however, have several stores, a school, and a small hospital.

The people of the back-country savanna and highlands wear tough clothing to survive the harsh climate. Durable cotton twill is used for clothing that must stand up to work on the farms and in the fields. Clothes must be light in color to reflect the intense rays of the sun.

Food is sometimes difficult to obtain in the back-country savanna. Many people live a long way from major railways and roads

*Village women sometimes share communal cooking and beer-brewing tasks. Chibuku, a beer made from corn, accompanies most meals in the countryside.*

that lead to the larger cities. In the 19th century, Europeans who lived and traveled in the harsher parts of the back country ate strips of sun-dried *biltong*—a kind of beef jerky or smoked meat that was easy to store for long periods of time. Biltong is still sold in Zimbabwe.

Most of the back-country communities practice subsistence farming, which means that the farmers can grow just enough to feed their villages. A staple dish of rural Zimbabweans is a hot and spicy meat stew. To quench their thirst, they drink *chibuku*, a beer made from corn.

Family life in the savanna and highlands is one of cooperation. Women cook and look after the mud huts where their families reside. Men work in the fields or tend cattle. Children are expected to help with the chores. On the larger farms of the highlands, families work together to keep the farm running. Men, women, and children are expected to help with all the farming chores, and people from nearby villages are often hired to work on the big farms.

Zimbabweans enjoy celebrating the numerous holidays of the country. The major holiday is the Independence Day celebration of

*Her baby on her back, a woman uses a pointed digging stick to prepare the flooded ground for planting.*

Zimbabwe's independence on April 18. Africa Day, on May 25, celebrates the continuing hope that someday all black African nations will be free, independent, and cooperative. Workers' Day, on May 1, celebrates the socialist workers of Zimbabwe; Boxing Day, a British holiday, falls soon after Christmas. Easter, New Year's Day, and Christmas are also celebrated.

## The Arts

The visual arts in Zimbabwe are a mixture of black African and European styles. Zimbabwe has some of the finest examples of African art; pottery and beads from the many ancient ruins are displayed in museums, including an exhibit at Great Zimbabwe. The Zimbabwe "birds," soapstone carvings found at Great Zimbabwe, are among the most famous artworks in the country. The rock paintings of the early tribes can be seen on the walls of rock shelters of the Matopos Hills. Other art forms include wood carvings, musical instruments, dishes, and figurines; delicately woven baskets for food and storage; and clay pots for eating and drinking. The mud walls of Ndebele huts are painted in traditional geometric designs.

*Traditional craftspeople produce finger-painted pottery and other objects both beautiful and useful.*

The European influence can be seen in art museums in Zimbabwe's larger cities. The most famous are the National Gallery and the Queen Victoria Museum in Harare. Most of the paintings found in these museums are works of famous European painters, such as the Dutch artist Rembrandt.

The larger cities have landscaped gardens, many of which were planted and designed by Europeans. The Ewanrigg Botanical Gardens have a collection of desert plants called aloes and one of cycads, which are fernlike plants similar to the giant ferns that flourished millions of years ago.

The Shona have traditionally been musicians. Shona kings "spoke" to their spirit ancestors through the use of special imperial drums, some of which measured more than 12 feet (3.7 meters) in diameter. Other musical instruments used in the country were the *chigufe*, or flute; the *nyere*, a reed instrument; and the *chipendani*, similar to a harmonica. Most were used in marriage ceremonies.

Today music in Zimbabwe varies from a classical symphony performed by a visiting orchestra in Harare to the music of a Shona storyteller's drums or the latest song on the radio. The College of Music in Harare is a well-respected music school.

Zimbabwe is exciting to archaeologists. More than a dozen stone ruins are found in various parts of the country. Great Zimbabwe is the largest; the second largest is the Khami Ruins on the banks of the Khami River, west of Bulawayo. Dhlo Dhlo Ruins and Naletale Ruins also are near Bulawayo. Other ruins are found in the eastern highlands, including the Mutoko and Nyahokwe ruins.

Zimbabwe has produced many well-known sports and cultural figures. The Zimbabweans have always had an interest in sports, from soccer and rugby to tennis. The Zimbabwe women's field hockey team, an all-white group, won the gold medal at the 1980 Olympics in Moscow. Several Zimbabwean runners have competed in world championships. In 1995, Zimbabwe was host to the All-Africa Games, and it is hoped that the Zimbabwe soccer team will someday play in the World Cup championships.

Several famous authors, including some of the black nationalist leaders, were born in Zimbabwe. Albert Luthuli was born in Rhodesia and later moved to South Africa. His activities in South Africa's black nationalist organizations won him fame, and in 1961 he was awarded the Nobel Peace Prize. In 1962, he published his autobiography, *Let My People Go*. Black author Wilson Katiyo returned to Zimbabwe after 1980, after being exiled by Ian Smith's government because of his political writings.

Henry C. Gouldsbury, a white writer in the early 1900s, was popular within the European community and wrote more than 10 novels and volumes of poems, including *Rhodesian Rhymes*. Doris Lessing, a white author who has become world famous, wrote several novels that drew on the racism that she observed throughout Rhodesia. Her first novel was *The Grass is Singing*; others include *African Stories* and *Children of Violence*. In 1992, Lessing published *African Laughter*, an account of her return home to Zimbabwe after 25 years.

*Construction and growth from the 1940s to the 1970s made Salisbury—now called Harare—one of Africa's most modern and Westernized cities.*

# A Country of Crossroads

Most of the cities and towns in Zimbabwe are the result of European influence in the 19th and 20th centuries. The African peoples who roamed the savanna and highlands before the coming of the British settlers built few cities, because most of them were nomads who followed their game herds around the country. It is true that Great Zimbabwe is centuries old and was one of the largest ancient cities, but most of the other cities in today's Zimbabwe were built after 1890. After Zimbabwe became independent in 1980, the names of many cities that had been founded by British colonists were changed to reflect the black African heritage. For example, Salisbury became Harare, and Fort Victoria became Masvingo.

About 69 percent of the population is rural, living in the countryside and small villages. Of these rural Zimbabweans, most are black. Most urban Zimbabweans, or city dwellers, also are black. The smallest population groups—the Europeans, Asians, and people of mixed blood—are concentrated around the cities, although some whites own large farms or country estates. The two largest cities are Harare and Bulawayo.

Harare is the business and government capital of Zimbabwe. It is located in the High Veld of northeastern Zimbabwe, in the province of Mashonaland. Many roads lead to Harare because it is a center of trade, commerce, and government. It is the oldest modern city in Zimbabwe; as Fort Salisbury, it was the site where the Pioneer Column ended its march.

Harare has a population of about 1,200,000. It covers close to 540 square miles (1,399 square kilometers) and is the site of the Zimbabwean parliament. The National Archives, also located in Harare, houses artifacts that reflect the country's early history. For example, the British Union Jack flag first raised at Fort Salisbury in 1890 is found at the archives, as are diaries and mementos of Cecil Rhodes and other figures in Zimbabwe's past.

The capital is a major center of sports activities, with places to watch or participate in horse racing, soccer, rugby, tennis, cricket, golf, and other sports. Automobile racing takes place at the famous Donnybrook track. Not far from the city, Lake McIlwaine offers sailing and waterskiing.

Harare's climate is ideal for trees and plants. Every street is lined with colorful trees, shrubs, and flowers. The climate has made the countryside around Harare one of the most properous and productive farming areas in the country, with just the right amount of sunshine for crops such as corn.

Bulawayo is the second largest city and is located in southwestern Zimbabwe, in the province of Matabeleland North. Its population is about 621,000. Bulawayo is the country's principal railway junction and contains more than 600 factories.

Bulawayo has a longer history than Harare. In the early 1800s, it was the main headquarters of the Ndebele ruler Lobengula. The Shona called the city GuBuluway, or the "place of killing," because of all the fighting for power that occurred in the area. When the

BSAC occupied the city in 1893, Lobengula set it on fire to stop the British advance and fled north.

The city quickly recovered from the fire, and soon the British developed Bulawayo as a major link between South Africa and Fort Salisbury. The streets of the city reflect its frontier past—the broad roads are wide enough to turn a cart or wagon around.

Today Bulawayo is a modern city much like Harare. Many of its main attractions are connected to its past. The City Hall, used as a hiding place by the white settlers during the war of 1896, contains many items of historical significance. The Railways Museum, in the National Railways headquarters, houses engines and other railroad machinery from the beginning of the 20th century. The State House just north of Bulawayo was built on the site of Lobengula's residence.

*Flower sellers mass their colorful wares on a shaded pavement outside Bulawayo's city hall.*

*Railroad lines helped make Bulawayo the industrial center of Zimbabwe.*

Bulawayo also has one of the largest natural history collections in Africa. The mammal collection at the National Museum includes 75,000 specimens and is one of the largest mammal collections in the Southern Hemisphere. In other parts of the museum are historic articles, such as pottery and statues, collected from the country's numerous ancient ruins.

In the 1990s Chitungwiza (formerly Seke) grew into the third largest municipality in the country. Primarily a residential suburb just south of Harare, it has a population of 274,000 and was one of the venues for the All-Africa Games of 1995.

The fourth largest city is Mutare (formerly called Umtali.) Mutare is located in eastern Zimbabwe, close to the border of Mozambique, in the province of Manicaland. The city lies in a valley surrounded by huge granite mountains. It has a theater, a concert hall, and several sports facilities. A small museum preserves examples of the city's past, complete with displays of horse-drawn carts and carriages and early railroad locomotives.

Mutare is one of the country's most colorful cities. Around Christmastime, fiery red flame trees line all the streets. Nearby, the La Rochelle National Trust, a home given to Zimbabwe by the late Sir Stephen and Lady Courtauld, contains acres of gardens with rare trees, shrubs, and orchids.

Another city is Nyanga, located in the province of Manicaland in the eastern highlands. Nyanga is an important farming community. Water from nearby Kyle Dam is used to irrigate sugar and citrus farms. Nyanga is the world's largest producer of lithium ore, a soft silver-white metal.

Nyanga is not a large city, but it is surrounded by some of the most impressive scenery in Zimbabwe. Mount Inyangani is 8,517 feet (2,593 meters) high and is the tallest mountain in the country; Pungwe Falls flows into Pungwe Gorge, one of the country's most dramatic and beautiful river valleys; and Matarazi Falls is Zimbabwe's highest waterfall.

Other smaller cities are located throughout Zimbabwe. The oldest European settlement is Fort Victoria, now named Masvingo, which was one of the forts developed by the Pioneer Column.

Marondera (formerly called Marandellas) is a small city southeast of Harare. It is an important producer of beef, dairy, and tobacco products and a growing industrial center. Many British settlers believed that the climate of Marondera was perfect, as can be seen by the concentration of European private schools established in the city. One of the most popular was the Waddilove Institution. Founded by Wesleyan missionaries in the early 1890s, it later became an important teacher training center.

Other small cities were built around a certain industry or agricultural product. For example, Chinhoyi (formerly Sinoia), with a population of around 45,000, is northwest of Harare and is a center of tobacco and copper production. It was also the place where the Rhodesian civil war started in 1966.

Towns and villages also grew up around railway lines. Rutenga, in southeastern Zimbabwe, was the first direct rail link to South Africa. Eldorado, a village just east of Chinhoyi, is the site of one of the last gold mines worked by the ancient Shona-speaking people. It is located on a major rail line to Harare.

## Transportation and Communication

The early native Africans traveled the country mainly on foot, perhaps with pack animals, or with canoes along the rivers. There was little reason to travel from place to place except to trade goods or to raid other villages. But by the 1890s the European settlers needed faster and more reliable means to import and export goods, food, and minerals. In addition, they needed to maintain communication with each other and with Great Britain.

The first real road in Zimbabwe was the Pioneer Column. But this road and other roads made by the settlers were often nothing more than muddy, difficult trails. Heavy seasonal rains washed them out.

It soon became evident to Cecil Rhodes that the transportation system of the country had to change. Rhodesia needed to bring in more immigrants; minerals and metal ores needed to be transported across miles of savanna to industrial cities and other countries; and crops had to be exported. He decided that railways were the best solution.

*Herders in a canoe urge their cattle across the Zambezi River.*

By 1892, the first two rail lines were started, linking Salisbury to Mozambique in the east and South Africa in the south through Bulawayo. Branch lines were soon added, reaching the major mining centers. The laying of the tracks through Rhodesia took many years and was a painful and laborious process. Diseases such as dysentery and malaria killed more than 1,000 workers.

More than 1,714 miles (2,759 kilometers) of rails serve Zimbabwe today, connecting the country to all of the surrounding nations. The rail lines are run by the state-owned National Railways of Zimbabwe and are used for passenger travel, exporting and importing goods from bordering nations, and transporting goods, such as coal for electrical power, within the country. As a landlocked nation, Zimbabwe depends on its railways for trade—as do its surrounding neighbors. In the late 1990s, the World Bank and other organizations planned to spend Z$700 million to modernize the rail system, repairing track and replacing steam engines and signals.

River transportation has never been extensively developed in Zimbabwe. The larger rivers are often unsuitable for navigation because of rapids or seasonal variations in water flow.

Transportation by motor vehicles is another means of getting from one place to another in Zimbabwe. Cars and trailers travel on the more than 56,700 miles (91,000 kilometers) of roads that crisscross the country. Half of the roads are made of tar or concrete, and the other half are unpaved. Bridges have also been built over the larger rivers, although many are often washed out during heavy rains.

One of the easiest ways to travel in Zimbabwe is by air. Air transportation in the country began in 1920 when a plane from South Africa landed in the city of Bulawayo. (It crashed the next day on takeoff.) In 1932, Imperial Airways became the country's first major airline, flying from Cape Town to several areas in Southern Rhodesia.

In 1933, Imperial Airways received money from the Beit Trust in order to organize the Rhodesia and Nyasaland Airways (RNA). The Beit Trust was a trust fund bequeathed to Rhodesia by a South African diamond merchant named Alfred Beit upon his death in 1906. The money was to be spent on a multitude of projects throughout central Africa; in the 1920s, it was used primarily to improve the transportation systems of various countries.

In 1940, the Rhodesian government took over the RNA, changing its name to Southern Rhodesian Air Services. In 1946, the airline became the Central African Airways Corporation (CAA), under the control of the three territories that later would form the Federation of Rhodesia and Nyasaland. When the federation disbanded, the CAA was divided into three separate national airlines, including Air Rhodesia for Southern Rhodesia.

Today Air Rhodesia is Air Zimbabwe. The airline operates several flights within Zimbabwe and to other African nations, with limited services to Europe. A few smaller airline companies also operate domestic services within the country.

In addition to developing many means of transportation, Zimbabwe has developed a communications system. Telegraph lines were built in 1891, just after Cecil Rhodes's Charter Company entered the country; they still are used today in the less populated areas. A postal system was established in Salisbury in 1892. Letters were first sent by horseback, then by rail. Today mail is carried by rail and by motor vehicle.

*Air Zimbabwe is the national airline.*

Newspapers began publication soon after the first Charter Company settlement. They were sponsored and written by the European settlers. During the fight for majority rule in the 1960s and 1970s, many black nationalist newspapers were started; among the most important of these were the *African Daily News* and the *Bantu News*. Some of these newspapers were banned by Ian Smith's government. In their place, the government published the *African Times*.

After Zimbabwe became independent in 1980, all newspapers became the property of the new government. They were incorporated into a state-run bureau called the Zimbabwe Newspaper Group. The group distributes the two main daily newspapers: The *Harare Herald* and the *Bulawayo Chronicle*, with a combined circulation of more than 400,000. More than 50 periodicals, or magazines, also are published and distributed in Zimbabwe.

Telephone service, though limited, came to Rhodesia in the late 1890s. The first telephone lines were mainly built to connect British military command with the many forts during the war of 1896. A public telephone exchange was established in Salisbury in 1898. Today there are more than 300,000 telephones in use, mostly in the cities. Few rural Zimbabweans have access to telephones. By the late 1990s, Zimbabwe's telephone system was in dire need of maintenance, and many calls failed to connect. The government hopes to introduce better technology soon.

Radio reached the country in the 1930s; television appeared in the early 1960s. The first radio and television broadcasts were in English. Today Zimbabweans receive programs in English or in various Shona or Ndebele languages. There are more than 890,000 radios and 280,000 televisions in the country. Most of the televisions are owned by people in the cities.

*Three enormous stoves provide hot air for the blast furnaces of one of Zimbabwe's steelworks. The country is rich in iron ore to feed its steel industry.*

# Resources and Economy

Zimbabwe's economy is based not on a single resource but on many resources. The country has vast mineral fields. Its industrial centers are some of the most diversified and productive in Africa. It is a rich agricultural and cattle-grazing country, and it supplements its income with a healthy tourism trade.

Southern Africa has always been a center of mineral wealth. Large deposits of minerals run in veins across many countries. One such deposit is found in the Witwatersrand gold region in South Africa. Another deposit—filled with rich minerals such as chromite and lithium—is the Great Dyke running from Belingwe in southern Zimbabwe to Sipolio in the north.

Mineral wealth was a major reason for the success of Cecil Rhodes's Charter Company during the late 1800s and early 1900s. Gold was the principal mineral mined in the country after the Pioneer Column marched into Mashonaland. By 1895, gold prospectors had staked more than 68,000 claims. Mining towns dotted the land. Most of the towns were connected by rail lines that brought in goods for the townspeople and workers for the mines and carried the ore from the mines. The most important minerals mined were gold, coal, tin, and chromite.

*Mine workers in the 1890s suffered from miserable living conditions.*

During World War II, Rhodesian mines became a major source of metals and minerals to support the British war effort. Mica, a clear, flat, nonmetallic mineral, was used for insulation and fireproofing. Iron and chromite were mined and used in the production of planes and weapons.

After the war, the demand for Rhodesian minerals varied. For example, asbestos is a fibrous mineral known for its fireproofing qualities. In the early 1950s, because of rising world demand for the mineral, asbestos replaced gold as the country's chief mineral product. But by the 1970s world demand for gold and copper increased, and demand for asbestos dropped when it was found to be hazardous to animal and human health.

Today Zimbabwe remains one of Africa's top mineral-producing nations. More than 50 different minerals are mined across the country. Gold is not as important to the Zimbabwean economy as it was in the early part of the 20th century. In its place are metallic ores, such as chromite, and nonmetallic minerals, such as coal.

Chromite ore is used for the production of steel and in electrical equipment; it is mined in Selukwe and Belingwe. Iron ore, mined

*Mica is mined not by digging but by prying away sheets of the flat mineral.*

at Redcliff in central Zimbabwe, is used for electrical equipment and steel production. Copper, used for electrical purposes, is mined in Chinhoyi. Lithium, an important metal in the production of aircraft, is mined in Bikita.

Zimbabwe is a major producer of coal, which is used for energy production. Coal is used to run the hydroelectric plant at the Kariba Dam, and coal from Zimbabwe mines is exported to other nearby nations. One of the largest coal mines in Africa is in Hwange, near the Zambezi River. Other coal reserves have been found in the south-eastern Low Veld, but the resources of this area have not yet been developed.

Another boon to Zimbabwe's economy is its industrial centers. During World War II, Rhodesia increased its industrial production. The number of steel plants increased along with the demand for this important metal. New textile, sugar-refining, and other smaller in-dustries developed because goods from Europe were scarce during the war. The Rhodesian people had to develop their own industries in order to survive.

The next boost in industrial production occurred during the decade when Rhodesia was a member of the Federation of Rhodesia and Nyasaland. Southern Rhodesia benefited greatly from the union. In particular, the building of the Kariba hydroelectric dam on the Zambezi River provided valuable electricity to the mining operations in the country. The asbestos, beryllium, lithium, and chromite industries boomed, and exploration for ores such as iron, nickel, tin, and copper increased.

The federation encouraged the growth of industry. The number of chemical and motor-vehicle assembly plants increased. Companies in other countries were encouraged to build factories in the federation, especially in Southern Rhodesia. Cities and towns constructed additional roads and bridges. New rail lines stretched from Bulawayo to Salisbury (now Harare). European immigration increased, and black African people moved from the back country to industrial towns in order to find high-paying jobs.

Today Zimbabwe's industry is still one of the strongest sectors of its economy. Harare, the capital of Zimbabwe, is the center of industry, with tobacco, textile, food processing, chemical, fertilizer, and vehicle-assembly plants. Bulawayo is the center of important meat-processing, textile, tobacco, metal-refining, and vehicle-assembly industries. Industries in Kadoma, in central Zimbabwe, include

*Early in the 20th century, workers hauled wheat from the fields in ox-drawn carts.*

*Workers water tobacco
seedbeds. Soon the
young plants will be
moved to the fields.*

cotton ginning and textiles. Mutare has paper mills, timber, vehicle-assembly plants, and chemical industries.

Agriculture has always been important to the economy of Zimbabwe and the survival of the people. The Shona and Ndebele people plowed their land by hand. Their main crops were millet, corn, citrus, yams, and rice. These were subsistence crops, produced in quantities sufficient to feed local populations. Tobacco and cotton were also grown, and the Ndebele produced enough grain crops to trade with other countries.

After the arrival of the European settlers, great farms were established throughout the country, especially in the eastern highlands. These huge farms were designed to produce large quantities of cash crops, or crops that could be sold for a profit, such as corn, cotton, tobacco, and tea. Cash crops were sold inside the country, but real wealth came from exporting these crops to other countries.

By World War II, Rhodesia was basically a land of white commercial farmers and black subsistence farmers. The war stimulated agricultural production. The number of farmers increased as immigrants from war-torn Europe entered the country. New types of farming equipment and the development of high-yielding strains of various crops increased the country's agricultural production.

Today agriculture is the main source of income for about 70 percent of the nation's labor force. The farming industry is still dominated by white landowners. The government's plans to buy up white-owned land and redistribute it to black farmers have been set back by cash woes and international opposition.

*Corn, here being stockpiled for export by train, is Zimbabwe's major crop.*

Corn is Zimbabwe's most important crop. More than 80 percent of the annual harvest is exported to other nations; the rest—more than a million tons—is consumed by the people of Zimbabwe each year. Cattle grazing is also an important part of the county's economy, and beef is one of Zimbabwe's major exports. Other important export crops are cotton, tea, and tobacco.

Several agricultural centers produce the bulk of Zimbabwe's agricultural output. The Mazoe Valley, in the northeast, gets its water from the Mazoe Dam on the nearby Mazoe River. The valley is a major source of many types of fruits and vegetables. The Hippo Valley in the southwest is an agricultural center for sugar, cotton, and wheat. The High Veld region is the center of tobacco farming. Zimbabwe is the world's third largest grower of tobacco, producing over 200,000 tons a year.

Forest covers 61.6 percent of Zimbabwe, and forestry is gaining economic importance. The hardwood forests of the west and southwest, along the Zambezi River, produce about 100,000 tons of teak and mahogany each year. These are exported, but other woods are harvested for use in local construction and paper industries. It is estimated that Zimbabwe is losing 1.5 percent of its forest each year.

Tourism brings several hundred thousand visitors to Zimbabwe each year, mostly from South Africa. The money they spend is a useful economic supplement. After 1980, safari operations increased, offering bird-watching, white-water rafting, game viewing, photographic tours, and sportfishing expeditions. More than 3,861 square miles (10,000 square kilometers) of the middle Zambezi River are part of the UN World Heritage sites—an effort to safeguard the major wildlife areas and cultural or historic sites of the world. The most popular tourist attractions are the Mana Pools and Victoria Falls. The government of Zimbabwe hopes to encourage an increase in tourism.

The economy of some smaller towns and villages is based on crafts. People make pottery, iron and leather goods, and textiles, either to sell within the villages or to be sold through dealers or in marketplaces in the cities. The Zimbabwe dollar (Z$) is the country's currency. It is equal to approximately $0.09 in U.S. currency and is divided into 100 cents. The annual income of an average household of 5.8 people is Z$9,164. The average family in Zimbabwe spends nearly a third of its income on food and clothing. Alcohol and tobacco, travel, housing, and fuel and utilities are the other major expenses.

The standard of living remains much as it was under the Smith government. Many whites and some blacks in business and the government earn incomes far above the average and live very well. But Zimbabwe has severe poverty, especially in the back-country savanna, where jobs are scarce. Unemployment is a major problem in Zimbabwe, at nearly 10 percent, because industry is not growing rapidly enough to provide jobs for the thousands of people who come to the cities each year in search of work.

*Zimbabwe is a young nation; more than half of its people are under age 21. Better education and higher rates of school attendance are essential to the country's development.*

# Government,
# Health, and
# Education

Zimbabwe is rich in resources; its future could be a prosperous one. To bring about such a future, however, the government will need to improve the country's internal stability, health care, and educational system. Education is especially important to develop the skills needed in a technologically growing nation.

Zimbabwe's legislative body or parliament is called the House of Assembly. It has 150 members, 120 of whom are elected by the general population for five-year terms. (All citizens 18 years of age and older are allowed to vote in these elections.) The remaining 30 Assembly members are governors, chiefs, and presidential appointees. A speaker and the nation's attorney general also serve in the Assembly.

The executive president, who is the country's head of state, is elected for a six-year term by the parliament. The president presides over the parliament and also acts as commander in chief of the armed forces. Most presidential decisions are based on the recommendations of the cabinet, a group of officials selected by the president to oversee the day-to-day administration of governmental business. The president and his government also control appointments of senior officials in various branches of the public service, such as the police and military.

Zimbabwe now has one major political party, the ZANU-PF (Zimbabwe African National Union–Patriotic Front), led by Robert Mugabe. In its various guises, this party has dominated both the legislative and the executive branches since independence, in part because opposition parties have tended to be weak and disorganized. The main opposition parties now include ZANU–Ndonga (a pro-business, regionally organized party, and the only opposition group with seats in parliament); the Forum Party of Zimbabwe (FPZ); and the United Parties.

The country's military forces consist of the National Army and the National Air Force, with a total of about 42,000 soldiers. Many of the soldiers are from either ZANU's ZANLA or ZAPU's ZIPRA forces and fought during the civil war. Officers are trained at Zimbabwe National Army Staff College. Zimbabwe's military suppliers include Great Britain, China, and North Korea. Those three countries have also offered military training, as have Pakistan and the United States. Overall, Zimbabwe spends about 3.5 percent of its gross domestic product on defense.

The judicial system is based on the Roman-Dutch system that was used in South Africa in 1891. The highest ruling court is the Supreme Court, based in Harare; it has three judges of appeal and one chief justice. The next court, the High Court, has 10 judges. Finally, regional and magistrates' courts are found in the smaller villages and towns.

The country is divided into eight administrative provinces. They are Manicaland, Mashonaland Central, Mashonaland East, Mashonaland West, Masvingo, Matabeleland North, Matabeleland South, and Midlands. The provincial capitals are Mutare, Mount Darwin, Harare, Kadoma, Masvingo, Bulawayo, Gwanda, and Gweru. Each province has a provincial governor who reports concerns of the province to the parliament. More than 1,200 local officials, called district councilors, are responsible for reporting problems within the provinces to the provincial governors of the parliament.

Zimbabwe's official anthem is "God Bless Africa." The Zimbabwean flag has seven stripes of green, gold, red, black, red, gold, and green. In the left corner is a white triangle with a gold Great Zimbabwe bird on a red star.

Health care is an important part of planning for the future. Zimbabwe has always been troubled with disease, especially in isolated rural areas where adequate clinics and education are lacking. Bilharzia (an infectious disease transmitted by water parasites), malaria, sleeping sickness, and typhoid have all proved difficult to eradicate. Moreover, by the late 1990s Zimbabwe faced a new kind of epidemic—HIV and AIDS. Over a million people are estimated to have been infected with HIV. A fourth of all pregnant women are thought to be HIV-positive. Often, the virus spreads because people are ignorant of the danger and of precautions they may take to avoid infection. At times the government also has chosen to avoid public discussion of sexual practices and drug use because of traditional taboos or prejudices. Many experts fear that the disease has yet to show its full extent in Zimbabwe and other parts of Africa, and its effects are potentially devastating.

*Hospitals and rural clinics provide free health care to those who cannot afford to pay for it.*

The government is trying to provide sufficient health-care facilities for all Zimbabweans. Health care is now available for everyone, and it is free to those who cannot afford to pay for it. The country has eight major hospitals and more than 1,010 rural clinics. Many British doctors left the country after Mugabe rose to power, but since the mid-1980s the number of doctors has increased to around 1,500.

The average Zimbabwean can expect to live only to the age of 42. Even before the advent of AIDS, which weakens the immune system, pneumonia and diarrhea were leading causes of death. The infant mortality rate is 73 per 1,000 births, which means that 73 of every 1,000 babies die in infancy. The natural growth rate of the population is less than 2 percent a year.

Education is a crucial factor in shaping the country's future. Zimbabwe is a nation of young people; more than half of the population is under the age of 21. Most children attend primary school, but only about half attend secondary or high schools.

Before the Europeans settled in the area, there were few schools in the country. Missionaries had set up churches in many villages with the intention of educating the natives about Christianity. There was no other reason for establishing schools, as natives did not need an education to work on farms or raise cattle.

*Hope Fountain, founded in Matabeleland in 1870, was one of many mission schools that introduced education to the region.*

Schools quickly followed European colonization. But the schools were racially segregated, and few blacks were allowed to share the benefits of the educational system. Private schools and missions were built mainly for the education of white children. Schooling was free for white children from ages 7 to 15, but blacks had to pay for their children's schooling, and few black families could afford the high price of an education.

During the civil war, some black Africans were wealthy enough to send their children to schools in other countries. Many of these foreign-educated blacks became leaders of the nationalist movement and the new government. President Robert Mugabe went to South Africa for his education.

Today the government controls the educational system. Its goal is to educate every Zimbabwean child. The Ministry of Education has abolished school fees. It is building more high schools, but needs loans from international donors to do so. In 1981, the year after the establishment of the new government, the number of children in school jumped from 800,000 to more than 1.3 million, even though school attendance is not required by law. Today there are almost 3 million students in primary and secondary schools, and 48,000 in vocational school or college. The literacy rate is 76 percent.

*Using a painted section of a broken wall as his blackboard, a teacher gives an outdoor lesson.*

Most of the classes are taught in English. But the government requires each student to take courses in the Shona and Ndebele languages and in agriculture. Students are encouraged to learn skills such as carpentry or plumbing. Basic courses include math, science, and history.

Primary school lasts nine years. High school is either a college preparatory school for six years or a vocational school for four years, depending on the type of curriculum the student chooses and the student's grades. The University of Zimbabwe, in Harare, is open to both black and white students.

Strengthening the educational system has not been easy for Zimbabwe because there are too many students to educate. Many students live too far from schools to attend regularly, and the periods of drought have further decreased attendance, particularly in areas where famine is rampant and every child is needed to work. There is also a lack of teachers.

In secondary schooling the nation's progress has been especially slow. Many students drop out of the educational system after primary school to find jobs on farms or in the mines. The main reason for this is that many black Africans who live in the smaller villages do

*Helping with the family's work keeps many children out of school.*

not believe education is necessary for their children. They have always fished, hunted, or farmed the land to earn their living; why do their children need to learn anything else? The government has had to convince the people that education of the young is necessary if Zimbabwe is to be more productive in the modern world. But traditions are hard to overcome, and many parents keep their children out of school.

*The flag of Zimbabwe was raised ceremoniously in front of the United Nations building in New York City in August 1980, when Zimbabwe became the 153rd member nation of the UN.*

# Challenge of the Future

Geography has placed Zimbabwe in one of the most desirable—and therefore one of the most fought over—regions of Africa. Early nomadic tribespeople were attracted to the area because it offered food, shelter, and a comfortable climate. Later, powerful Bantu states mined the area's gold and built great stone structures, such as those at Great Zimbabwe. Later still came Cecil Rhodes's Pioneer Column and the beginning of the European influence. White settlers made fortunes in the fertile highlands and the mines of the savanna. But the entrance of the settlers, followed by the formation of the British colony of Southern Rhodesia in 1923, paved the way for racial discrimination, decades of struggle for majority rule, and a bloody civil war.

Southern Rhodesia prospered under white rule. In 1952, it joined two other British colonies to form the Federation of Rhodesia and Nyasaland. The federation lasted for only 10 years, because 2 of the member nations demanded independence from British domination and government by their black African majorities. Southern Rhodesia remained a white-ruled British colony, almost surrounded by independent nations governed by their black majorities. In 1965,

Prime Minister Ian Smith illegally declared Rhodesian independence. The black majority population was still discriminated against; the whites continued to reap economic and social benefits. For 15 years, the white government forces and the black nationalists fought a civil war. Eventually, the pressure from the black people and the rest of the world was too much for Ian Smith's white minority government. In 1980, Zimbabwe was born—a republic governed by its black African majority.

Today Zimbabwe is more prosperous than many African countries. But there are problems as the Zimbabweans try to cope with a program of economic change that will succeed only with careful planning and outside aid. Zimbabwe's transition from a socialist to a market economy means a time of high inflation, a devalued national currency, unemployment, and great debt from international borrowing to build business. Zimbabwe's economy must also weather unpredictable factors such as drought as its government tries to project confidence and discipline.

Zimbabwe is in the midst of a rapidly changing Africa. Its neighbor, South Africa, has established universal suffrage and elected a former political prisoner, Nelson Mandela, as president. But other nearby countries, such as Rwanda and Zaire, have continued to experience bloody internal unrest. Zimbabwe has survived its own crisis of ethnic conflict. It now has a newly stable trading partner in South Africa, and both countries are focusing on development and investment.

Zimbabwe is a member of the United Nations and of the Organization for African Unity (OAU), which promotes unity and cooperation among all the African nations. Zimbabwe is also a member of the African Development Bank, the World Trade Organization, the Non-Aligned Movement, and the Southern African Development Community, which coordinates development projects in the region.

Zimbabwe is working to be active in the affairs of Africa and the world. But its real challenges are internal. Railways, roads, industry,

*Children in a refugee camp greeted the announcement of Zimbabwean independence with gestures of pride and power.*

and agriculture must be maintained. People must be taught the managerial skills needed to maintain existing businesses and develop new ones. Unemployment, which in the late 1990s stood at about 10 percent, must be limited, and conservation programs will be needed to protect resources such as forests and wildlife. Another major crisis facing Zimbabwe is twofold: health and how to afford it. Drought and famine have always been concerns, but the crisis of AIDS, and the specter of a tenth of the population becoming ill, is a huge problem at a time when Zimbabwe is trying to build and finance a future.

Still, there is hope for Zimbabwe. It is one of the richest countries in Africa. Agriculture, mining, and industry have given it a good start for further development. With time, money, and education, Zimbabwe can position itself to become a major force in the regional and international market, luring investors and tourists and keeping skilled people employed and healthy.

# ◄ GLOSSARY ►

| | |
|---|---|
| **archaeologist** | A scientist who studies ancient human civilizations. |
| *baobab* | A bulky tree in the savanna of Zimbabwe with thousands of short, thin branches resembling the roots of a tree. |
| *biltong* | A beef jerky made in Zimbabwe. |
| **Charter Company** | First known as the British South African Company, this was the company contracted to develop mining in Mashonaland under the British government. |
| *daga* | Mud huts built by many of the natives in the savanna. |
| *indaba* | Shona for "meeting." |
| *laager* | Dutch for "army encampment." |
| *lobola* | A "bride price" traditionally paid by an African groom to the father of the bride. |
| *mambo* | A Rozwi ruler in the 1600s. |
| *marula* | A tree whose fruit is especially enjoyed by elephants. |
| **Pioneer Column** | A group of more than 500 men who marched from South Africa into Mashonaland to settle or look for gold and other minerals; the Column disbanded at Fort Salisbury in September of 1890. |

| | |
|---|---|
| Rhodesia and Southern Rhodesia | Former names of Zimbabwe. |
| *rinderpest* | A fatal disease in cattle that spreads rapidly if not controlled. |
| socialism | A political system that holds that the wealth of a country should belong to the entire population and be administered by the state; in a socialist system, the people work according to their abilities and receive compensation based on their needs. |
| subsistence farming | Producing just enough food to feed a single family or village. |
| Unilateral Declaration of Independence (UDI) | The 1965 declaration of Rhodesia's independence from Britain. |
| *veld* | Dutch for "field." |
| ZANU | Zimbabwe African National Union, originally a black nationalist group and then a political party. Before its 1989 merger with ZANU, it was composed almost entirely of Shona-speaking members. Its military unit was known as ZANLA, or Zimbabwe African National Liberation Army. |
| ZAPU | Zimbabwe African People's Union, originally a black nationalist group and then a political party composed of Ndebele-speaking members. Its military unit was called ZIPRA, or Zimbabwe Independent People's Revolutionary Army. |
| *zimbabwe* | Ruins, literally "stone houses." |

# ◄INDEX►

## PICTURE CREDITS